Scott —

Dream Big!

THE POWER OF CONSISTENCY

PROSPERITY MINDSET TRAINING FOR SALES AND BUSINESS PROFESSIONALS

WELDON LONG

WILEY

John Wiley & Sons, Inc.

Published by John Wiley & Sons, Inc., Hoboken, New Jersey.
Published simultaneously in Canada.

For general information about our other products and services, please contact our Customer Care Department within the United States at (800) 762-2974, outside the United States at (317) 572-3993 or fax (317) 572-4002.

Wiley publishes in a variety of print and electronic formats and by print-on-demand. Some material included with standard print versions of this book may not be included in e-books or in print-on-demand. If this book refers to media such as a CD or DVD that is not included in the version you purchased, you may download this material at http://booksupport.wiley.com. For more information about Wiley products, visit www.wiley.com.

Library of Congress Cataloging-in-Publication Data:

Long, Weldon, 1964-
    The power of consistency : prosperity mindset training for sales and business professionals / Weldon Long.
        p. cm.
    Includes index.
    ISBN 978-1-118-48680-1 (cloth); ISBN 978-1-118-52658-3 (ebk);
    ISBN 978-1-118-52653-8 (ebk); ISBN 978-1-118-52625-5 (ebk)
        1. Success in business. 2. Selling—Psychological aspects. 3. Motivation (Psychology) I. Title.
    HF5386.L767   2013
    658.3'1245—dc23

                                                    2012038551

Printed in the United States of America

10 9 8 7 6 5 4 3 2 1

Success in sales and business ultimately comes down to how well and how often we do the little things. It's not about closing one huge deal every now and then. It's all about doing the small things on a consistent basis. Do the little things well, and the big things will happen.

CONTENTS

FOREWORD

Since we don't get to take advantage of the power of 20/20 hindsight, we humans grow by making mistakes, learning from them, picking ourselves up, and carrying on. Sometimes the mistakes we make are so big that the task of picking ourselves up seems impossible. The key to improvement is in recognizing the error of our ways, finding a better course of action, and being consistent in moving in a more positive direction. Weldon Long understands this better than most. He has studied and boiled down hundreds of concepts into one simple principle: To improve your life in all respects, design your course and then embrace consistency.

I'm honored to write this foreword for many reasons, primarily because I can relate so well to the topic. You see, I've made my fair share of mistakes. I quit college after 90 days. I failed my real estate exam several times. However, I repeatedly and consistently studied and took it over and over again until I passed.

I made only one sale my first six months in real estate. I kept working hard at it, but as it turned out, I was working hard at the wrong things. When I was down to my last $150 in savings, I was directed toward the world of self-development. My eyes were opened to unbelievable possibilities. I became a real student for the first time in my life. Through a whole lot of trial and error and a great deal of consistent effort, I achieved a tremendous level of success in my career.

During my last year in real estate, I sold 365 properties—the equivalent of one home per day. I wouldn't have been able to serve that many clients if I hadn't been consistent in the level of service I provided. Today, I am fortunate to have taught literally millions of others, sometimes in groups as large as 18,000 people, how to avoid the mistakes I made.

Upon meeting Weldon Long and learning about how he overcame mistakes far greater than my own, I knew I wanted to help this man get his message out to the world. I have had the pleasure of sharing the stage with him at my sales training seminars. Even after hearing his story many times, it still strikes an emotional chord deep inside me. The passion he has to serve others so that they can learn from his mistakes—and from his subsequent journey to success—is immeasurable. Knowing him today, it's hard to imagine him living the life he did in his past.

I'll never understand why so many of us do this, but we often wait until we hit rock bottom before we even begin looking for a better way of living our lives. Weldon Long dug himself a much deeper hole to climb out of than I ever did, but I'll let him tell you that story. What you really want to learn from him is how and why he made those decisions to make his life better. He learned the necessary lessons from his failures. He took the actions required to make his dreams come true one step at a time. He's a regular guy with an incredible story that will make the challenges you face in life seem like a walk in the park. I have tremendous respect for him.

You can gain all of the education in the world, but if you don't become the person you need to be to achieve the greatest benefit from that education, you might as well have stayed in kindergarten. Had I not learned how to develop myself as a person as I was learning the business of real estate, I would have lost or squandered the fruits of my labors. I had to work hard to overcome negative self-esteem hits from my past and to stop listening to my own self-defeating thoughts that I was not good enough, that dropping out of college had ruined my life, that I wasn't a good student, and that I would never make it in real estate because I was too young.

If I hadn't learned how to envision myself as a worthy individual, to see selling as an honorable profession, and to view my youth as giving me an edge with younger home buyers, I probably would have failed miserably for much longer than I did—and I would have given up. I would have added "quitter" to the long list of negatives describing the patterns in my life. Instead, I worked diligently at my craft and became a top-selling agent.

Weldon Long's journey from failure to success is nothing short of inspirational. Yet he doesn't just share his story in this book. He teaches you very simple and straightforward steps to implement in your own life.

To become a better person, salesperson, employee, or employer than you are today, you need to understand how to create personal change in your life. If you don't, the life you live will depend on the whims of others.

Learning about business and about sales and marketing is crucial. But, to achieve real success, you need to first see yourself in your mind as a successful person. Some might call this self-esteem or refer to it as your self-image. The point is that it's up to you to choose the life you want to live, envision it, and then build it.

At my company, we have been teaching selling skills and strategies since 1976. We often use a triangle to demonstrate the three fundamental types of skill required to achieve success in a selling career or as an entrepreneur. The base or foundation of that triangle includes four attributes: attitude, enthusiasm, discipline, and goals. This book is a unique and powerful representation of all four of those critical, fundamental skills.

You won't succeed in business or with your personal relationships if you don't have the proper mindset. If you have been deemed a loser and a failure your whole life by others or by the thoughts you allow to exist in your mind, it won't matter how many business and sales strategies you learn. You will always be limited by your beliefs about your core personality. In other words, to get your sales and business life right, you have to get your head on right first. The principles in this book will help you do just that.

The Power of Consistency contains so many pearls of wisdom that I stopped counting. Weldon Long invested a great amount of time and effort to simplify what others have taught as very complicated subjects. Even after personally working with some of this type of information for years, I found myself truly enjoying his take on it. Weldon brings high and mighty psychological principles down to earth so that you can benefit from their implementation in your own life in a very simple, yet powerful manner.

There's a saying by legendary football coach Vince Lombardi that applies here: "The only place the word 'success' precedes 'work' is in the dictionary." You can read, listen, and learn all you want, but until you put into practice the knowledge you have gained, nothing will change. Five years from now you'll be the same person, living the same life. In fact, you may have lived each year just like the last. Weldon outlines for you exactly *what* to practice and *how* to practice it to gain the most benefit from the strategies he used.

The subtitle of this book indicates that it's geared toward sales and business professionals. Although I'm confident you will find it beneficial if those are your chosen careers, I believe the message within these pages is destined for a much greater audience. After all, *everyone* is in selling. We sell ourselves every day to every single human being we encounter (and even a few nonhumans, such as our pets). This list includes our loved ones, our neighbors, and our friends, the people we encounter in the coffee shop, on the freeway, and, of course, during the course of our business lives. And we can all benefit from *The Power of Consistency*.

If you take Weldon's message to heart, if you embrace the knowledge he has to share, you can, in way less than five years, be the person you've always wanted to be, living the life of your dreams and having all the rewards you deserve. Once you reach that level of success, you will aspire to even greater achievements than you can imagine today. This may sound like a pipe dream to you now, but I challenge you to put Weldon's strategies to work for just 90 days and see how powerful they really are.

—Tom Hopkins, author of *How to Master the Art of Selling*

ACKNOWLEDGMENTS

Very special thanks to my chief operating officer (COO), Doug Wyatt, who has been my alter ego for the past six years and somehow tolerates my temperamental nature while making me appear smart and sane. It's a tall order, but he does it beautifully.

Many thanks to my smart and talented marketing and video production staff, Dale Warner and Andy Mitchell, for making me look like I know what I am doing.

Special thanks to Kevin Small at Result Source, and all the wonderful folks at John Wiley & Sons for making this thing happen. Also, many thanks to "the speaker in the sneakers," David Behr, for making our live events happen all across the country.

I owe an endless debt of gratitude to the late Dr. Stephen R. Covey for his kindness and generosity and for writing *The 7 Habits of Highly Effective People*, which forever changed the course of my destiny. His passing was met with the sadness of millions of admirers around the world. Dr. Covey was one of most influential leaders of the twentieth century. He was also profoundly influential in my life, as his work saved me from certain self-destruction. In 2009, I was privileged to meet and work with Dr. Covey after he endorsed my first book, *The Upside of Fear*. Somewhere out there, Dr. Covey is making the angels better leaders. He will most certainly rest in peace after having left this world significantly better than he found it.

A very special thanks to Laura Oien, Judy Slack, Michael Hansen, and everyone at Tom Hopkins International for their help and support. Of course, a special thank you to the legendary Mr. Tom Hopkins for his support and example of how a true professional carries and conducts himself. Thank you, Tom—you are most certainly the real deal.

Thanks as always to my mother, Mary Goodeau, and to Eloise Ilgen (aka Nana) for their love and support and always accepting my collect calls from the joint. Also, I would be remiss if I didn't recognize Janet Cole for her support over the years, without which my story may have been a very different one. Janet, you are a sterling example of how a woman maintains her dignity and class despite the vicissitudes of life.

My love, devotion, and gratitude to Taryn and Skylar, who gave me the missing pieces to the puzzle of life. You inspire me every day to be the man God meant me to be.

And finally, a super-duper very special thanks to my son, Hunter, who has been my constant and unwavering source of inspiration and has made me so very proud to be his father. Son, you have made me a better man, and I love you more than words can adequately express. Matti is a lucky girl.

INTRODUCTION

Circumstances do not make the man, they reveal him.
—James Allen

O*nce upon a time* there was a man who had destroyed his life by the age of 32.

And although what so many people claim is true—that you can measure a person's character by how he responds when the chips are down and his back is against the wall—there was nothing in this man's life to suggest he was even remotely prepared to overcome the challenges before him.

But you never know what someone can accomplish if he or she wants it badly enough.

On June 10, 1996, this individual stood motionless in a prison cell—a cell indistinguishable from so many others that had served as his home for more than six years—devastated over the recent news that his father had died. He looked deeply into the eyes that glared at him through the scarred stainless steel mirror in his tomb.

Through the initials scrawled by unknown tenants before him, he saw the reflection of an unemployed high school dropout and a three-time loser who had spent his entire adult life in this hopeless state of despair. For as long as he could remember, he had known only prison, poverty, and struggle. He had no money, no hope, and by all accounts, no future. He had never held a steady job or owned a home, and he'd abandoned his three-year-old son. He had never done an honorable thing in his life.

As he stared at his pathetic countenance, grieving over his dead father, the son he'd left behind, and the life he'd essentially wasted, he considered the words of Ralph Waldo Emerson—who he had just discovered:

"We become what we think about all day long."

He concentrated on these words and repeated them to the man in the stainless steel reflection.

"We become what we think about all day long."

He thought about the words intently as he gazed into his own miserable reality. Upon staring at his reflection, he noticed that he was getting old. He noticed lines on his face that he hadn't noticed the day before. His teens and twenties had raced by at warp speed. And where was he now? Growing older before his very eyes. How had this happened? How had he allowed things to get so out of control? And the most pressing question—was it too late to do anything about it? After all, he wouldn't see the streets again until he was nearly 40 years old.

He considered Emerson's words once more:

"We become what we think about all day long."

Again he asked himself, Was there more to life? What would it take to find out? Was he even remotely capable of altering the course of his seemingly forged destiny? Was it actually possible to *become* something different merely by *thinking* something different?

Despite seemingly insurmountable odds, he decided to find out.

He set out on a journey of creating a plan for his life—something he later came to call his prosperity plan. He focused his thinking on a productive, meaningful life and on taking actions that aligned with these new thoughts. Although the prospect of changing his life by changing his thoughts seemed somewhat preposterous, he was desperate enough to give it a shot. He even became obsessed with this notion—that he could alter the course of his destiny simply by thinking about things differently.

And he did.

By the time the man was released from his third and final trip to the penitentiary seven years later, he had earned a bachelor's degree and an MBA in management. In 2002, just one year before his release, he was also credited with saving a prison guard's life.

Despite the overwhelming obstacles and adversity, he went on to build a life of wealth and integrity. He reconnected with his son and raised him to become a remarkable young man. He started a small company from scratch and grew sales to $20 million in just 60 months, earning it a spot on *Inc.* magazine's 2009 list of the fastest growing privately held companies in America. He purchased beautiful homes in the mountains of Colorado and on the beaches of Maui.

He shared his story by writing a memoir called *The Upside of Fear: How One Man Broke the Cycle of Prison, Poverty, and Addiction,* which won numerous awards and which personal and organizational development titans Dr. Stephen R. Covey and Tony Robbins endorsed. He eventually became one of the county's most powerful and dynamic speakers. He shared his work with the Napoleon Hill Foundation and luminaries such as Mark Victor Hansen. He shared the stage with legendary sales expert, Tom Hopkins, and taught countless sales professionals the process he used to transcend 25 years of poverty and misery and create an exceptional life of business success.

Despite being the underdog of all underdogs and the longest of long shots, he created a life of honor and prosperity.

I know this man's story well—because it is my story. I am that man. *I am Weldon Long.*

After spending more than two decades of my life failing and struggling—and spending 13 of those years behind concrete walls and razor wire—I emerged a transformed man and built the life I once dreamed about in a cold prison cell.

My life and business were forever altered by *The Power of Consistency*—a force so powerful it can move mountains and completely transform the fortunes of men, yet so subtle it's easily and often overlooked. I used *The Power of Consistency* to bring myself from a life of poverty and desperation to one of wealth, happiness, and peace of mind.

It is the one thing that changed everything in my life and business, and I am going to share a simple, step-by-step process to help you create new levels of success in your sales and business career.

The Problem

Every sales and business professional faces challenges and adversity that they can—and frequently do—use to justify their mediocre or poor performance. Perhaps your challenges aren't as severe as the ones I faced, but everyone has their issues, right? No one gets out of this deal alive, and no one gets through a sales and business career without hitting a few bumps and earning a few bruises along the way.

Whether your challenge is a slow economy, cheap competitors, no access to capital, worthless leads, unqualified customers, or a boss you'd like to meet in a dark alley, everyone has something—or several things—keeping him or her from wealth and prosperity. And if you are waiting for these obstacles to magically disappear so that you can be wealthy, you might as well get used to being broke. They're not about to pack up and move on to make your life easier. You have to find a way to succeed and prosper despite them.

The only real question is whether you are going to let the obstacles put a boot in your ass or whether you are going to put a boot in theirs.

Successful sales and business professionals are not successful because they somehow avoided obstacles. They are successful because they have mastered the art of creating a prosperity mindset that is geared and programmed to overcome any challenge and thrive in the face of adversity. A prosperity mindset is the key to the kingdom. It takes you to a place where the streets are paved with gold.

The bottom line is that *shit happens*. We all know it. But if you want to succeed and prosper in sales and business, then you had better nip the complaining in the bud and find a way to prosper *despite* the challenges and adversity.

You can't just wait for your luck to change, the economy to improve, your competition to raise their prices, or "better customers" to walk through your door. You'll be waiting a long time if you do.

Whether it's an economic, competitive, or personal issue that's threatening your sales and business performance, just remember the words of famed *Saturday Night Live* character Roseanne Roseannadanna: "It's always something."

The key to winning in sales and business is to create a mindset that compels you to thrive and grow in the face of adversity. It requires that you identify just one or two things that ensure success and do those things—consistently. It's about kicking the challenge's ass . . . not waiting for things to magically get better.

And here's some news for you: *You already know what to do* to create wealth and success in your business. You just aren't doing it on a consistent basis. If you were, your sales career and business would be exceptional, regardless of the difficulty you face.

Are you surprised by the claim that increasing the number of prospects you contact would increase your sales? Would you be shocked to learn that if you improved your "closing sequence" and got better at identifying problems and recommending solutions to your clients, you would dramatically increase your income?

I seriously doubt that either of these things is news to you. You already know these activities would improve your sales performance and income. You just aren't doing them on a consistent basis.

You see, overcoming obstacles and creating wealth is not a problem with lack of information; it's a problem with lack of action. *You just aren't doing the things you know you should be doing on a consistent basis.*

Odds are that you've made some attempts to do these things—you're given it the old college try—but then little things seem to get in your way. And although you temporarily make some improvements, it's not long before you find yourself falling back into your old routine. You can't seem to make the changes stick or to consistently *do* the things you already *know* you should be doing.

For example, you know that you need to call your customers more often to retain them. But after doing it for a few days, you stop making the extra calls. You either don't have time, or something else gets your attention—and eventually a more aggressive competitor wins your customers' business.

You know you need to decelerate the sales process and take more time with your prospects before recommending solutions. And you even take this approach a few times. But before you know it, you are hurrying through the process again and "dropping off bids."

You know you need to do a better job of finding new customers and may even spend a couple of days prospecting like there is no tomorrow. Yet after that initial burst of activity, you quickly revert to your old ways of taking orders and waiting for someone to call *you.*

You know you need to spend more time with your prospects explaining why your products and services are better than your competition's and why you are worth a few ~~hundred~~ bucks more. You even have a couple of great calls, but soon you are back to matching your competition's low prices and complaining that no one cares about quality and service.

You know you need to study and implement a better sales and closing process to grow your revenue. You even look into some new training, but ultimately you decide to wait. Before you know it, you are kicking yourself in the backside as you leave an appointment without formally asking for the order, knowing you let a great opportunity slip away.

Welcome to the conundrum of human nature—*knowing exactly what you need to do to increase your sales and grow your income but not doing it on a consistent basis.*

Most of us know what we need to do to succeed and are aware that we've got to work harder and serve better to compete in this day and age. But we're just not doing those things consistently. The people who are making the most money don't *know* anything the people making the least money don't know. They are just doing more of what they need to do—and therefore getting ahead of the ones who are not.

This book will help you defy the conundrum of human nature by compelling you to *habitually do the things you need to do* to realize wealth and success in your sales and business career.

I can promise you that I didn't overcome years of despair and build an Inc. 5000 company that generated $20 million virtually overnight because I'm luckier or smarter than anyone else. I did it by establishing and operating according to a prosperity mindset that drove me to do the things I needed to do—*every single day*. It wasn't rocket science or brain surgery. It was just plain old hard work.

This book will help you duplicate my success. Sales and business success is not a question of *whether* you should create a prosperity mindset; it's a question of *when*.

The Power of Consistency makes the simple proposition that we tend to take actions that are consistent with the things we repeatedly say to ourselves. Our sales and business activities are a reflection of our thoughts and expectations. In essence, it states, "Private affirmations dictate future actions." You will see throughout this book how this subtle yet limitless force can alter anything in your life and business—and how "private affirmations" will dictate your future actions *and your future results*.

Using this powerful yet invisible force will allow you to overcome whatever challenges threaten your sales and business success and instead prosper in the face of any adversity.

This approach is guaranteed to lead to prosperity, because you simply cannot do the right things in your life and business on a consistent basis and accidentally create the wrong results. Of course, this doesn't mean you won't face occasional short-term challenges and setbacks. What it does mean is that you will ultimately create the sales and financial results you desire.

Although it's a somewhat depressing fact, most people have failed to do the things they know they should be doing to get their lives on the right track. The people who are taking consistent actions are the exceptions—exceptional professionals who enjoy exceptional sales and business results.

But we see them all the time, living life on their terms as we complain about the forces acting against us. We see them shining in their companies and careers as we struggle to get by. We watch as they earn incomes that provide a life of financial security, while we fight to make ends meet.

We watch the years roll by—always longing for a better life, yet feeing a better life is just beyond our reach. We know what we need to do. We just aren't *doing it* with any reliability.

But regardless of the external challenges and adversity, we all have within us the ability to create wealth, happiness, and peace of mind. As Emerson wrote, "What lies behind us and what lies before us are tiny matters compared to what lies within us."

You already have everything you need to create the life and business you deserve. *The Power of Consistency* will help you harness what lies within you so that you can create a brighter future for you and your family, despite the challenges you face along the way.

If you and I were sitting together right now and I asked you to describe your professional and financial goals, you could probably identify them pretty quickly. If I asked you to list two or three things you needed to do to make each dream a reality, you could quickly figure that out too. But what if I asked you, "Why aren't you doing them?" You'd probably respond with "I don't know."

Again, the conundrum of human nature: knowing exactly what you need to do to increase your sales and grow your income but not doing it on a consistent basis.

But exceptional sales and business performance is well within your reach. You just need to follow a simple process to create your prosperity mindset—and let that mindset drive you to do the things that lead to wealth and prosperity. As a result, you can become exceptional.

The best part is this: the things you need to do to be exceptional are downright simple! That is, in fact, why most people don't do them; they frequently seem insignificant and not even worth the effort when you look at them individually. But their cumulative effect is incredibly powerful.

The Solution

The question remains: How *exactly* do you use *The Power of Consistency* to overcome challenges and adversity and create wealth and prosperity in your sales and business career? Well, it takes creativity and consistency. Fortunately, that's what this book is about.

To overcome any challenge and create transformational results in sales and business you need to get your mind right and develop a prosperity mindset that is geared and programmed to transcend any obstacle.

The truth is that the world's most successful people think differently than others—and think about different things.

Within these pages you will learn how to leverage *The Power of Consistency* in your sales and business career by getting your mind right. You will walk step by step through the process of creating a prosperity plan and learn how to drive consistent action toward that plan through a daily quiet-time ritual. You will also learn how to leverage cognitive dissonance to keep yourself on track and doing the things you know you need to do.

You will learn that your life is a perfect reflection of your thoughts and the things you repeatedly say to yourself. And once you master this process, you will find that external forces have very little to do with your business and sales success. You will learn that if you believe you will succeed, you are right; and that if you believe you will fail, you are also right. You will learn that your *expectations create the ceiling on your results*.

You will learn a four-step process called the upside of *FEAR* that involves:

*F*ocus
*E*motional commitment
*A*ction
*R*esponsibility

The FEAR process will guide you through the steps of creating a personal prosperity plan and give you the tools you need to transcend obstacles and adversity. You will learn how to get *focused* on what you want and how to become deeply *emotionally committed* to those things. You will learn the value of a quiet-time ritual and how to take consistent *action* toward reaching your goals. And finally, you will learn how to take *responsibility* for the decisions that define you when faced with the inevitable challenges in business.

By implementing these ideas and taking actions on a consistent basis, you will transcend the conundrum of human nature. You will become one of those rare people who know what you need to do to create wealth and prosperity, and you *will actually do it.* You will become exceptional, and the possibilities for your business will become endless.

And perhaps most valuable, your success will come from within. It won't depend on external conditions such as a better economy, better leads, better customers, or a better boss. Your success will emanate from within a better *you*, regardless of peripheral challenges.

Think about it. If a knucklehead like me can use *The Power of Consistency* to go from the dregs of existence to a life of unimaginable wealth and happiness, how much further can *you* go using the same process? Any challenges you face will likely pale in comparison to the adversity I created for myself—and had to overcome to achieve personal, professional, and financial independence. Odds are, you are infinitely better off today than I was in 1996. So if I can experience these amazing results, imagine what you can accomplish.

You can go *a lot* further than me. In fact, I have only scratched the surface of what is possible. You have the opportunity to build on what I have discovered and take your understanding to a higher level as you create success and help others do the same.

A Few Words about Implementing This Process

Nothing will change once you have mastered the concepts that *The Power of Consistency* teaches—that is, if you don't implement what you have learned on a consistent basis.

A few years ago, I was speaking with the chief operating officer (COO) of one of the world's leading training organizations. I asked him to identify the single biggest challenge facing his company and the legion of companies using his training systems. His answer was simple: "*Implementation*. If our clients would just use the training they purchased from us, they would see unbelievable improvements in growth and productivity." But of course, they didn't.

Sales executives and professionals of all backgrounds all face the same challenge: understanding that success is not a knowledge problem, but rather a consistency problem.

During training, attendees typically get excited about the prospect of selling more and earning better incomes. They're often bouncing off the walls with new enthusiasm. Unfortunately, after a few days, the inevitable distractions of life and business cause some to forget everything they learned. And before they know it, the new sales concepts and system are collecting dust with the other sales training programs that didn't work.

The Power of Consistency will help create exceptional sales and business results—but *only if you consistently implement them*. It is a comprehensive process that virtually guarantees better results as you move through the steps.

Why This Book?

I decided to write this book for two reasons.

First, it would not make sense for me to go from a life of desperation and poverty to a life of wealth and affluence and *not* tell others how I did it. There is absolutely no reason everyone cannot enjoy the same success I have enjoyed.

This book isn't about something I read or think *might* work. This book is about the lessons I learned on the mean streets of real life and real business, and I feel that it's my responsibility to share what I have learned with others.

The second reason is because of chance encounters I had with two extraordinary men: the late Dr. Stephen R. Covey, author of *The 7 Habits of Highly Effective People*, and the world's leading expert on transformation and change, Tony Robbins.

Allow me to explain.

When my father died on June 10, 1996—the day I began my journey to prosperity—the first book I picked up was *The 7 Habits of Highly Effective People*. When I read the profound wisdom within those pages, I felt as though Dr. Covey was speaking directly to me. I realized, of course, that literally millions of others felt the same way. Yet somehow his words resonated with me on a level I had never before known.

It seems pathetic looking back that I was examining the core principles of life for the very first time at 32 years old. Nevertheless, as I read Dr. Covey's book, a vision for my life began to take shape. I began to feel hope and optimism despite the utter chaos and misery that defined my life behind prison walls.

The year after I read *7 Habits*, I was transferred to FCI Florence, located in the Federal Prison Complex in Florence, Colorado. In the library I found the key to put what I was learning into action. That key was Tony Robbins's *Personal Power* program. As I listened to Tony Robbins over the next 30 days, I realized I must not only create a plan for my life—but more important, I must take *action!*

I began putting what I had learned into practice over the next several years. Although my transformation is testimony to the work of many brilliant thinkers and writers—including Dr. Wayne Dyer, Napoleon Hill, Viktor Frankl, the incomparable Tom Hopkins, and others—none were more influential than Dr. Stephen R. Covey and Tony Robbins.

Many years later, in 2003, I was released from the penitentiary and sent to a halfway house for wayward convicts. I arrived there with nothing more than a dream and the determination to succeed. Over the next few years, I created a life that was a surprise to everyone except me—since I had seen this new life in my mind for many years.

In 2008, I wrote the manuscript for a memoir that I titled *The Upside of Fear*. Shortly thereafter, I began to contemplate who I would like to endorse the book, and two luminaries came immediately to mind: Tony Robbins and Dr. Stephen R. Covey. Never mind that these were the two biggest names in the field of personal and organizational development in the last 30 years and I was a nobody, thrice-jailed loser. I had learned that being practical when it came to dreams was unnecessary.

In December of that year, I added two new components to my personal prosperity plan when I wrote, "Tony Robbins and Stephen R. Covey have endorsed *The Upside of Fear*." I also included this affirmation to my daily quiet-time ritual and came to believe it would happen, despite having no (rational) reason to think I would ever meet these men or gain their endorsements.

Nevertheless, a few months later—thanks to an unlikely conversation that began on Twitter—Tony Robbins agreed to allow me to use his Twitter comments about my story as an endorsement for *The Upside of Fear*.

What I found especially remarkable was the words he used to describe my story. Although there were many ways to define my journey, Robbins wrote, "Congratulations on your turn-around from prison to *contribution*."

He did not say, "Congratulations on your turnaround from prison to prosperity or wealth or success." He chose to acknowledge and recognize my *contribution*.

When I read his words, I realized the most important part of my story is the opportunity it gives me to help others. This book is part of that contribution.

And that lesson was solidified even further when I met Dr. Stephen R. Covey.

During the early months of 2009, my public relations team tried to contact Dr. Covey for an endorsement. Months went by and we were unable to make any progress. Eventually we came up against the date for the final hard-copy printing of *The Upside of Fear.*

At about that time I was invited to speak to a small group of business leaders at their monthly luncheon in Colorado Springs. Just before I was introduced, a man stood up at the front of the room and announced, "As most of you know, my daughter works with Dr. Stephen R. Covey. They will be in town next month, so if anyone here would like to meet Dr. Covey, let me know before you leave today."

I could hardly believe what I was hearing. My team and I had been trying for months to reach someone close to Dr. Covey. And here was the opportunity to meet the man himself, presenting itself before me.

I mentioned several times during my presentation the profound influence Dr. Covey had on my life. Afterward, the man who had announced Dr. Covey's trip to Colorado Springs approached me and offered to get an advance copy of my book to Dr. Covey. He also offered to make arrangements for me to meet the man whose words so dramatically changed my life.

I couldn't believe it. I would finally have the chance to meet Dr. Covey face to face. And if he read my book—and *liked* it—I just might be able to get him to endorse it.

A month later I sat and listened in stunned amazement as Dr. Covey discussed the 7 *Habits* principles that had so profoundly affected my life. After the presentation, I had the chance to meet Dr. Covey.

I came up empty as I searched for something intelligent to say during our interaction. Sensing my struggle, Dr. Covey smiled and said, "I loved your book."

Sounding like the kid from Fat Albert, I said, "I ba lobed your book ba too ba." I'm pretty sure spittle was running down my chin.

Since I knew there was no way I'd be able to pull it off, I decided at that moment to stop trying to act cool. Quite the opposite, in fact; as I stared into Dr. Covey's eyes, I was overwhelmed by emotion and began to weep. Dr. Covey looked at me, and recognizing my struggle, he put his arms around me and hugged me.

He then stepped back, looked deep into my eyes, placed his hand on my heart, and declared, "You have a divine destiny." He repeated the words two more times: "You have a divine destiny. You have a divine destiny."

"Wha?" I stammered.

"Your story," he continued. "You have a divine destiny to share your story to help others."

Holy cow! I thought. Is he kidding? Am I hearing things?

We spoke for a few more minutes—and then it was over. But I couldn't get his words out of my head. As Dr. Covey walked away, I contemplated how much my life had changed since I first read his words in a cold and lonely prison cell.

A few days later, Dr. Covey agreed to endorse *The Upside of Fear*.

Perhaps most striking about this entire series of events is that Dr. Covey wrote the endorsement on June 10, 2009—13 years to the day that my father died and I decided to change the course of my destiny.

I am profoundly grateful for the kindness and generosity that Tony Robbins and Dr. Stephen R. Covey showed me. They had nothing to gain by going out of their way for me—only something to give.

These two stories—of how these two men came to endorse *The Upside of Fear*—illustrate two things.

First, they highlight this book's central theme: thoughts are incredibly powerful things, and making a specific thought and visualization part of a daily quiet-time ritual can lead to exceptional and unexpected results in life and business.

Second, they convinced me that I must share my story and what I have learned with others. I feel a deep sense of responsibility to share with you exactly how I beat the odds and turned my life around so that you might do the same in your own life, despite the myriad of challenges that face every one of us.

I hope you find that this book makes a valuable contribution to your life and business. I hope you will also use it to discover and reach your divine destiny.

This book will teach you the simple yet powerful process of *The Power of Consistency* that transformed my life and business. You will learn how to go from knowing to doing. You will understand and harness what lies within you to create amazing results in your life and business.

This book is not the definitive word on business and personal development. It's not the definitive word on anything, in fact. There are many brilliant thinkers and researchers on the subjects of success and personal achievement. I am not one of them.

These are merely my personal and professional experiences and the lessons I learned that changed everything in my life. I don't have reams of research backing my methods. I do have hundreds of amazing stories from clients who have overcome challenges and prospered in the face of economic, business, and personal adversity.

Wealth and prosperity in your sales and business career are closer—*much* closer—than you may realize. In fact, wealth and prosperity are just a thought and a consistent action away.

That is the essence of *The Power of Consistency*—taking consistent actions that are congruent with what you repeatedly say to yourself and watching those actions create amazing results in your business regardless of external realities.

Welcome to an amazing journey of creating success and prosperity in your sales and business career. Welcome to *The Power of Consistency*.

CHAPTER ONE

Think *Inside* Your Box

Get Your Mind Right

We become what we think about all day long.
—Ralph Waldo Emerson

To fully leverage *The Power of Consistency* and generate massive sales and business results, you must begin by understanding the concept of getting your mind right. This basically requires that you become clear on a very important point: Whatever fills the space between your ears will eventually escape the boundaries of your mind and show up in your life and business—for better or for worse.

This isn't magic, voodoo, or some kind of mysterious "secret"; it's just a reflection of human nature, as you'll see in later chapters. The weakness with many books on the subject of the power of positive thinking or the law of attraction is that they seek to discuss this thought-becomes-reality concept in mystical or existential terms. But it's just a reality of our neurological system that translates a thought into a result.

When I first came across Emerson's statement that "we become what we think about all day long," I was sitting in a prison cell—and quite honestly, I found it preposterous. How in the world could my thoughts define my results in life? It all seemed a bit too much like smoke and mirrors; I needed something a little more pragmatic. Like my papaw Wainwright used to say, "I'm from Missouri . . . *show me!*" (I don't think my papaw Wainwright was actually from Missouri, which made his use of the axiom rather odd.)

Then one day it dawned on me that, somehow, all the chaos in my head had escaped my brain and manifested in my life. What I was living perfectly reflected what I was thinking.

Once I processed the implications of this "living what I was thinking" thing, I realized *I alone* was therefore responsible for my life's quality and results. Of course, it was a little overwhelming at first, realizing that I had created a miserable life for myself.

But soon I became excited about it; after all, if I "thought" myself into this awful reality, I could certainly think myself into a more positive one. It was liberating. It wasn't likely that my life would improve because I somehow became smarter or my luck changed. But if my life could improve by changing my thoughts… hell, even a bonehead like me could change those!

Here is what I figured out sitting in a 9×7 cell with way too much time on my hands:

Imagine you have a box sitting in front of you holding everything you need to build a beautiful motorcycle. There are no missing or extra parts in the box. There are *only* the parts you need, nothing else.

Now imagine that you also have the tools and mechanical skills necessary to assemble this beautiful creation. You begin the process of removing the parts from the box one by one.

As you do so, you put them together according to the mental image you have of how this machine is supposed to look once it's finished. Part by part, piece by piece, you assemble your masterpiece.

You aren't putting the pieces together randomly; you are doing so systematically according to the picture of a motorcycle you have in your mind. In other words, you don't bolt the wheels on the handlebars. You put the wheels—and everything else—where they are supposed to go.

Now imagine that you stay focused on completing the assembly. Nothing distracts you from your mission. You maintain laser focus on assembling everything according to your master plan.

Each piece that you empty from the box serves as the foundation for the next. You bolt the engine to the frame and the carburetor and gearshift to the engine. You attach the throttle, brake, and clutch cables to the engine components they control.

And eventually, all your hard work comes to fruition. You step back and admire your creation as it glistens in the sun.

You've used every part; the box is now empty of its contents. The final product stands assembled before you.

Now ask yourself a simple question: Once you have emptied the box's contents and assembled them in perfect accordance with your thoughts about what a motorcycle should look like, what are the chances that you would look up to see that you have accidentally baked a cake?

"That's impossible!" you might say. "There is no way I could *accidentally bake a cake* when I had only motorcycle parts in the box. I pulled out only what was in the box, and I put the parts together piece by piece according to my vision of a motorcycle!"

Your common sense tells you that it's impossible to create anything except what was in the box. And your common sense would be absolutely correct—because you cannot focus on creating what's in the box and *accidentally* create something else. If you have only motorcycle parts in the box and assemble them according to your mental picture of a motorcycle, you can create only a motorcycle. You cannot accidentally bake a cake.

You might be wondering at this point what any of this has to do with the underlying concepts of this book. In essence, the box is a metaphor for your mind. And whatever is in your mind is coming out—just like the motorcycle parts—but in the form of a million thoughts, attitudes, beliefs, choices, and decisions. Eventually, whatever comes out of your mind will form to create a perfect reflection of whatever was once in your mind.

The results you experience—in sales, business, and life—are not accidents. They are reflections of whatever is in your box. And whatever is in your box is an accumulation of a lifetime of thoughts, attitudes, beliefs, choices, and decisions. In much the same way, whatever is in your mind—your thoughts, attitudes, beliefs, choices, decisions, and expectations—is *all* you can create. You can't visualize and create one set of results in your mind and accidentally create a different set of results in your physical reality.

This is why you cannot focus on creating abundance, prosperity, and excellence in your business and accidentally create scarcity, struggle, and mediocrity. In fact, you can generate negative results such as these only if they have somehow found their way into your box. Over the course of your sales and business career, you accumulate *expectations, thoughts, attitudes, beliefs, choices, and decisions*. Although your box's contents are technically invisible, they are as real as anything in your physical (and visible) world.

You remove these expectations, thoughts, attitudes, and beliefs through the countless choices you make throughout your life and career. Those decisions accumulate to create your results. That's why your success and prosperity in sales and business are a perfect reflection of whatever is in your box.

Sometimes other people such as our family members (especially parents), put things in the box for us. Sometimes our community and neighbors, coworkers, and competitors put things in there too. We can even accumulate stuff from talking heads on television and through the information we read in a book or see in a movie. Sometimes we put things in the box ourselves.

It doesn't matter how all these things got in there; it only matters that they are there—and will eventually come out in one way or another. Regardless of who put them there, everything in your box forms your belief system. They help to form your basic view of the world and what you expect from yourself and others.

Then, over the following years and decades, you remove the parts from the box—piece by piece and part by part, just like the motorcycle parts. And just as you did with the motorcycle, you assemble those parts according to your mental image and expectations of how your business should look. Each piece serves as the foundation for the next—and then eventually all of your hard work comes to fruition. You create a final product as a result of your master plan, all of which comes together according to your thoughts and beliefs about your business. You step back and admire your creation. Only this time, it's not a motorcycle; it's your sales and business results.

You've used every thought and belief and have emptied the box of its contents. You stand back, take a deep breath, and behold the business you have created—a perfect reflection of whatever was in your box.

Now ask yourself the same question you did when you were finished with your motorcycle: Once you have emptied the box and assembled its contents perfectly in accordance with your mental creation, what are the chances that you would look up to admire what you have built only to see that you have accidentally created something that was never in the box?

Not very likely, right? Because as we've already found out, everyone's business is a perfect reflection of what they have in their minds. For each person, there was only one type of business that could have been created—and it was not an accident.

This, of course, means that *you* are entirely responsible for your business's quality and condition, because you alone have 100 percent control over what goes in your box. Even though some of its contents were put there when you were a child, one of your jobs as an adult is to choose what stays and what goes. You can be a hoarder, or you can clear out the clutter and get focused and organized. It's absolutely your choice.

Your business is not a reflection of your past struggles and difficulties, so don't even try to blame your parents, your ex, a mean boss you once had, or anyone or anything else. Your thoughts and beliefs are completely under your control, and they are *completely* your responsibility. If your business doesn't look the way you want it to, take a long hard look within yourself. What thoughts, attitudes, and beliefs are poised to come out of your box and create your results?

Although this realization may be a little hard to swallow at first, the implications should actually excite you. After all, if your results in business are a reflection of luck, what are the odds your luck will suddenly change? If they're a reflection of your past, how on earth will your past ever change?

But if your business results are simply a reflection of your thoughts, what are the odds you *can* change your thoughts? It's not even a matter of odds; it's a certainty. You can start to turn things around immediately—as in right this minute. That's the beautiful part of accepting responsibility for the quality and circumstances of your business: coming to the realization that you can change it. If someone or something outside of you is responsible, you are at its mercy. But nothing external can determine your results—unless you choose to allow that. If victimhood is in your box, then victimhood is all you can take out.

Therefore, the first step in creating a prosperous career is evaluating what's in your box. Then remove any "junk" and replace it with whatever results you really want by exercising dominion and control over what you tell yourself on a consistent basis. This is the essence of getting your mind right.

Socrates said, "An unexamined life is not worth living." I suspect the historians and philosophers will cringe when I say this, but I think Socrates was suggesting that we all need to take a long, hard look at the "junk in our trunk." It's not an easy process, but it's a necessary one.

After my father died in 1996, I knew I had to make a change. I knew what I needed to do to stay out of prison and build a productive life: stop breaking the law, get a job, and take care of my son. Apparently, I was getting arrested and going to jail because I was breaking the law. I wasn't going to jail because I had bad luck or because someone was out to get me. These consequences were clearly the result of my actions.

It wasn't about something I didn't *know;* it was about something I wouldn't *do.* I knew what I needed to do to create a better life. I just wasn't doing it regularly.

I realized that the only way to change my destiny was to change what was in my box. So I started reading the great writers and philosophers in an attempt to discover exactly what the contents of my box were—and to figure out how to change it.

Soon, I stumbled across a passage written by Friedrich Nietzsche, who quoted the universal law that, "We attract that which we fear." When I first considered those words, I thought they were preposterous. Why would I attract things in my life I did not want? It seemed ridiculous.

But later, I was perusing passages in the Bible when I came across a scripture where Job proclaimed, "For the thing which I greatly feared is come upon me, and that which I was afraid of is come unto me."

I thought it was odd that two men separated by philosophy and thousands of years were essentially saying the same thing. Was it possible that I could create things I did not want in my life simply by thinking about them? Could I actually attract things that I was afraid of just by holding onto them in my mind?

Eventually, I came across a book called *Man's Search for Meaning* written by Viktor Frankl, where I read these simple, yet powerful, words: "Fear may come true."

After stumbling across this concept for the third time, I had to stop and consider how it might be influencing my life. I thought about it, finally acknowledging that what I feared most in my life was going back to prison, losing my son, being homeless, and being a loser.

And that was exactly how my life looked. That was exactly what I had attracted.

I had created a life that was a perfect reflection of what was in my box and what filled my mind. Somehow all the chaos and fear in my peanut-sized brain was getting out of my head and showing up in my life.

This realization was profoundly liberating, because I had always thought my life was just a consequence of having really bad luck. Once I realized that it was just a product of my miserable thoughts, I was ecstatic, because I could control my thoughts. And that meant I could change them for the better.

And so I did. When I changed my thoughts, I changed the way I felt. And when I changed the way I felt, I changed the way I acted. And all of this led me to create better results.

As I came to appreciate my newfound power over the results in my life, it occurred to me that most of the sources I was learning from attributed our ability to create amazing things to ethereal and mysterious sources. But the reality that our lives are perfect reflections of our thoughts is not exclusively a metaphysical or spiritual concept. This is the case because of a simple physiological process whereby our minds generate thoughts that lead to chemical secretions that lead to emotions that lead to actions that lead to results. It really isn't all that mystical, nor is it a mystery.

The following is a simpleton's explanation of how it works.

A thought goes into your box, which generates a chemical that triggers an emotion. The emotion results in a particular action, which creates a result in your life. Therefore, the result you experience is ultimately a reflection of the initial thought—due to the physiological process you underwent. And that process—repeated a gazillion times over your lifetime—creates a certain quality of life.

The quality of your thoughts determines the quality of your life. That's why Emerson said, "We become what we think about all day long." That's also why the fearful thoughts that inhabited my box eventually manifested themselves in my life. The invisible eventually becomes visible, and my fearful thoughts triggered fearful emotions. Those in turn led me to take unhealthy actions, which created results that mirrored the fearful actions.

It's simply a reflection of how our neurological and physiological systems work together to create whatever is in our box.

So I made a decision in 1996 to empty my box of destructive and limiting beliefs and replace them with thoughts and beliefs that would create an exceptional life. I started this process by outlining what a perfect life for me would look like.

Keep in mind that most all of what was in my box was bad—really bad: violence, destruction of self and others, poverty, and entitlement. I had to empty it *completely* and start from scratch. Your situation is likely somewhat different than mine. Odds are that there is a lot of good stuff in your box as you begin this journey. You won't need to empty all of it, like I did, just a few of the nagging issues that are holding you back. I, on the other hand, had to gut that bad boy right down to the studs. And as I outlined what an exceptional life for me would look like, I dreamed big.

I took a piece of paper and wrote down the things that defined a perfect life for me. I then stuck that paper on my cell wall with toothpaste. Over the next seven years, I focused on that list every day. I committed emotionally to achieving the items on it. And I began taking actions daily that were consistent with the things I knew I wanted.

I put a new life (thoughts and beliefs) in my box, and eventually, through a million small decisions and choices, I pulled that new life out of my box. For example, I began filling my box with "I am an awesome father to my son," "I am wealthy beyond my wildest dreams," and "I am a man of honor, character, and integrity." (The remainder of this book will detail how I created and deposited these new thoughts and beliefs in my box.) Within a few short years, everything on that list came to pass.

As I began to experience the amazing life that I had been forming in my mind, I realized the entire process was fairly predictable. It was just a matter of how my brain, thoughts, and emotions worked.

Many of us struggle to understand this process because half of it is invisible. If we could see it, perhaps it would be easier to process and understand. But the fact remains that we *can't* see the most important things taking place in our lives, because our thoughts and emotions are invisible.

The following basic process explains why our thoughts become our lives:

Your thoughts *drive your emotions. Your* emotions *drive your actions. Your* actions *drive your results.*

You might have expected it to be more complicated than that, but it isn't.

Your thoughts send a signal to a part of your brain called the hypothalamus, which secretes a chemical that triggers an emotion. The emotion leads to an action that eventually leads to a result. That is basically what determines the quality and circumstances of your business.

The actions accumulate and result in your life. That's why your business results are a mirror reflection of your thoughts.

Whatever goes in the box eventually comes out and creates your business. You put things there or allow others to. You pull them out. And that's it—for better or for worse.

Now consider this: Your emotions and actions are reflections of your thoughts—so even if the thoughts are inaccurate, the emotion that follows is real. And because the emotion is real, the actions and results are likewise real. Therefore, it is completely possible to create a real emotion and a real action based on an entirely false thought.

Consider the following powerful example: Several years ago, two teenage girls were involved in a horrible automobile accident—so horrible, in fact, that law enforcement could not tell which girl was which. The two girls were of similar size, hair color, and appearance, and the cops who came upon the scene could not tell them apart. To make matters more complicated, one girl died and the other survived.

Eventually, the families and officials sorted out the confusion. One family went to the hospital, and the other family went to the morgue. The families' grief was unimaginable. Both were inconsolable.

Think about how each family felt. The family at the morgue was overcome by grief, loss, and unimaginable pain. The family at the hospital—while feeling a glimpse of gratitude that their little girl has survived—was still overcome with worry and anxiety.

Consider how these powerful and intense emotions affected each family's actions. We can rarely separate what we feel from what we do, and we certainly can't separate what we do from what we get. The result is a direct reflection of our actions.

But here is where things get really weird.

After one family had a funeral and the other family went to the hospital, everyone realized a terrible mistake had been made. The daughter of the family that had planned a funeral was alive in the hospital. The daughter of the family that went to the hospital had actually died. Everyone had gotten the girls' identities wrong. Because both were so badly injured, these accident victims had been wrongly identified.

Now ask yourself a simple question: Were the emotions and actions of each family the result of what was real—or what *they thought* was real?

Of course, it was the latter. The family that thought their daughter was alive experienced the emotions of a family whose daughter survived. It did not matter that their daughter had actually died. Their gratitude and relief mixed with worry came as a result of what *they thought* was true.

The family that thought their daughter had died experienced those associated emotions: grief, anger, despair. It did not matter that their daughter had actually survived. They felt according to what *they thought* was true.

Although the tragic circumstances are likely quite different from anything any of us has ever known, this story has a critical lesson for all of us. It forms the foundation on which you can better understand what drives your actions and business results.

Your business results are a reflection of your actions, which come as a result of your emotions. Your emotions are a result of *what you think is true.*

So if you think the economy sucks, that thought will incite emotions and eventually actions that will drive results consistent with a bad economy, even if your initial thought about the economy is wrong or inaccurate.

Imagine a sales professional who has surrendered to the mistaken belief that he cannot succeed in a sluggish economy and that clients care about only price, without regard for quality or service.

Once the sales professional has that thought, a signal is sent to his hypothalamus, which triggers an emotion consistent with the thought. What do you suppose that emotion will be? Enthusiasm? Optimism? Excitement? Not very likely, is it?

In fact, the emotions likely experienced will be hopelessness, anxiety, and an expectation of failure. In that emotional state, how is the sales professional likely to *act?* More than likely, the emotion will foster a lackluster and half-hearted sales presentation.

The result, of course, is predictable. The prospect is unimpressed with the product or service as a result of the sales presentation and makes a decision based solely on price. Ironically, as the sales professional mopes back into the office, he proclaims, "I knew it! I knew these lousy customers didn't care about our quality and service. They care only about a cheap price!"

Through his own thoughts and expectations, the sales professional has generated the emotions that drove his actions that created the expected result.

If you think your customers don't care about quality and service, then you will feel and act according to this assumption, even if your initial thought about your customers is wrong or inaccurate.

Now here is the kicker: The exact *opposite* of this is also true.

If you think the economy is good, that thought will create the emotions and actions that will drive results consistent with a good economy, even if your initial thought about the economy is wrong or inaccurate.

Imagine a second sales professional who has the basic thought and expectation that because the economy is sluggish, it is more important than ever for her customers to make a good purchasing decision. She believes that because the economy is slow, her customers demand a higher level of quality and service from suppliers.

Her thoughts trigger emotions of optimism and excitement as she reviews the superior quality and service her company offers over lower-cost competitors. Her excitement and enthusiasm fuel a dynamic sales presentation, and it comes as no surprise to her when the prospect catches her passion and belief and awards her the business. Again, the results are predictable.

Her thoughts and expectations generated the emotions that triggered her enthusiastic actions, which created her expected results. Just as her defeated coworker finishes his woe-is-me speech, she walks into the same office and exclaims, "I knew it! I knew our customers valued quality and service more than ever and are willing to pay a few extra bucks for it!"

If you think your customers care about quality and service and are willing to pay a few extra bucks for it, that thought will create the emotions and actions that will drive results consistent with customers who care about quality and service, even if that initial assumption was wrong. Your emotions are not always a reflection of facts or what is actually true; they simply manifest what you believe to be true. What you think isn't always consistent with the facts and objective reality. And because of this, reality is sometimes irrelevant.

However, regardless of the veracity of our thoughts, they *will* eventually dictate our emotions, actions, and results. In much the same way, your business will become a reflection of what you believe to be true. Remember: You can pull out of the box only whatever is in the box. As long as you believe it, it is in the box. And anything you put in, you will eventually pull out.

The bottom line is this: When you have a thought that you believe to be true, your brain will send a signal to your hypothalamus, which will emit an emotion, which begets an action, which will create a result, which will define the quality and circumstances of your life and your business.

Everyone has a metaphorical box that follows him or her around in life. Thoughts, ideas, beliefs, dreams, and expectations go into the box, where they mature. We eventually retrieve these as we develop and grow professionally and make decisions about our careers and businesses.

It is crucial to remember that the relationship between thoughts, emotions, actions, and results is a *linear process*, one that always occurs in the same order. Thoughts come first based on our life experiences, perceptions, and expectations. Emotions come second, and actions, third. Finally, a result is created.

Thoughts → Emotions → Actions → Results

It's also important to remember that the first two steps are *invisible*, whereas the second two are quite visible. This is important, because we tend to put a lot more emphasis on the part we can see: a particular action and the result.

For instance, you may observe someone who seems to be creating a pretty miserable life for himself. It's very easy for others to say, "Well, look what he is doing!"—because this person's actions and results are visible to others. However, it's much more difficult to see—and therefore, to understand—the emotion that's driving the action and the thought that's driving the emotion. The fact that things are invisible to us frequently leads us to diminish their importance. The answer seems obvious to us: This person should stop doing the things that are creating his poor quality of life.

But until he changes his thoughts, he will not change his emotions. And until he changes his emotions, he won't change his actions. And until he changes his actions, he won't create better results.

Our tendency to focus on what we can see—and ignore what we can't—causes us to grow continually frustrated with ourselves or others for not having the lives we want. This is precisely why we've got to spend more time understanding and shaping what we can't see before we can change what we can see. We've got to understand what's in the box.

Imagine someone telling you that she is bound and determined to change her results in life. She is ready to create a superior existence that includes a successful business. She is committed to reaching new levels of wealth, happiness, and prosperity.

Now imagine that this person said she was not willing to do anything differently. She wants a different life, but she's not planning to change her actions in any way to get it.

Wouldn't this be an absurd expectation? We all know that the only way to get better outcomes is to start doing something differently.

However, here's the rub (and I think you know what's coming): You can't generate better results without changing what you do (actions). *But* you can't change what you do without changing what you feel, and you can't change what you feel without changing what you think.

In other words, you have to start at the beginning, to look past the visible to the invisible. You have to look deeper than the results and actions.

Albert Einstein said, "We cannot solve our problems with the same thinking we used when we created them." This is why actions alone will never produce new results. We must alter the actions' source: our thoughts.

Your sales results and career can be exceptional. My life is a stark example of the fact that no matter how far we have fallen, we can get back up and do amazing things. No matter how bad things are, they can get better. No matter how many mistakes and bad choices you've made, you can overcome them and start making new and better ones.

Changing how you think will change the way you feel, and you'll begin to act upon these enhanced feelings, all of which will lead you to generate better results in your sales and business career. And when you see these amazing things in your business, you'll know they are not the result of luck or accident. Rather, they are the product of your thoughts.

It is helpful as we analyze what's in our boxes to understand where the existing junk in our trunks came from. Being able to identify its source makes it possible to begin exercising some discernment to ensure more junk does not find its way in there.

Junk sneaks in from many sources, especially when we are young. Usually the stuff in our box very closely resembles the stuff in our family's box, since we frequently believe the same things our family believes. Our thoughts and beliefs are pretty much a reflection of what those around us—especially those who raised us—think and believe. We tend to see the world the way our community, society, and family see it.

When we are young, people just walk by our boxes, throwing junk in. For instance, my dad used to say things like, "We can't afford that! Who do you think we are, the Rockefellers?"

I also remember my dad telling me, "Rich people are crooks." Those were beliefs and thoughts he had accumulated over his life, and without ever realizing it, he put his junk in my trunk by repeating those beliefs to me over many years. Eventually those things found a way out of my box and were created in my life.

While it may be impossible to "forget" limiting beliefs, you will learn in this book how to overpower the limiting beliefs with new, empowering beliefs.

Think about what you learned about sales and salespeople when you were young, as well as what others around you believed. Did you adopt many of the same beliefs?

We've doubtlessly heard at some point that we can't trust salespeople or that they'll rip you off in a heartbeat. Think about the stereotypical used car salesman. We hear about tricks and scams salespeople use to get their grubby little hands on our money. We hear about "snake oil" and the smoke and mirrors salespeople use to sell it.

Are these some of the thoughts in your box? Did you adopt any of them? Imagine the difficulty you will have prospering in a sales career if, deep down, you don't even *like* or *trust* sales professionals. How can you possibly excel at something that you don't respect? How can you become an expert in sales if you're worried about your family judging you for it?

We will examine your fundamental beliefs about sales and business as we work through this process. We'll replace any of the junk in there with more empowering beliefs, which will pave the way for improved sales and business performance.

Even as adults, we still accumulate some junk. Have you ever spoken to someone at work who spends most of the day lamenting about how bad things are—and then ended up agreeing with that person? If you ever find yourself stuck in one of those conversations, you are putting that person's junk in your trunk.

If you believe that prospects care about only price, what do you suppose you will pull out?

On the other hand, what if your box is full of beliefs that people still long for quality and service and that they are willing to pay a few extra dollars for them? What do you suppose you will pull out?

Of course, you can't ignore your coworkers or avoid the news. However, you *do* have to be aware of the sources of the junk so that you can decide what gets in and what stays out.

Your results and outcomes in business will never exceed your expectations. For example, what are the odds of pulling a 200k annual income out of a box full of 50k expectations? Thus, you have to be careful that the information going in your box is not undermining your success by limiting what you think is possible. This process will show you how to identify the junk in your trunk—and what to do about it.

The key is to make sure that whatever is in your box is a product of design, not default. That's how I turned my life around. I put new stuff in my box and spent the subsequent years pulling that stuff out.

I created this book as a guide for you to create your prosperity plan and learn to review it during a quiet-time ritual. That's just a fancy way of saying this book will teach you how to eliminate the crap from your box, put some way better stuff in there, and then pull it out to create the sales and business results you deserve.

I think it's important that I explain the information in this book in a very simple, practical way. These concepts have been around for a long time, but sometimes people discuss them in a way that confuses or complicates them unnecessarily.

From my years as an entrepreneur, business owner, and sales professional, I have learned a very simple lesson: the confused mind says "*no!*" So if folks are going to use this information, I believe it's necessary to make it simple. There is *no need* for the mystery.

You'll probably find as you work through this process that your sales and business career looks a lot like your thoughts about it—simply because of how your neurological system works. Chances are that you're rarely surprised by your performance, since it's pretty much consistent with your expectations. It's nothing mysterious; it's just Mother Nature.

Once you understand how your thoughts get re-created in your business, you will know exactly how your career got to where it is today. You will be able to see how the thoughts that inhabit your skull have manifested themselves in your business.

You will also notice and understand that the process by which thoughts drive emotions, actions, and results is a very predictable pattern, and you will come to understand the source of many of these lackluster results.

You will see their genesis in your thoughts—for better or for worse.

Remember the quote from Emerson: "We become what we think about all day long." As you work through this book, you will come to understand why Emerson was right. You will understand how the invisible eventually becomes visible via a predictable and dependable process. You will learn to depend on your understanding of how to use this process to create the sales and business results you need and deserve. You will have the tools to create wealth and reach new levels of sales and business performance.

In the next chapter, I will discuss a little part of your brain called the reticular activating system, which is largely responsible for your business becoming a reflection of your thoughts. After that, we will begin the process of examining what's in your box—and figuring out how you can change it.

CHAPTER TWO

Congratulations! You're Right! . . . Even When You Are Wrong

Why be happy when I can be right instead.
—Weldon Long

Have you ever driven from your office to your home without ever consciously thinking about driving? Think about it: You managed to safely operate your 2,000-pound car and navigate traffic, follow traffic signals, and make it to your destination—all while being distracted with a gazillion other things.

Your kid calls and tells you to hurry up so that she isn't late for soccer practice. Then an employee beeps in to tell you he is going to skip the sales meeting tomorrow. Just as you finish with that, your wife calls to remind you to pick up a gallon of milk and a stick of butter from the grocery store.

All the while, you're weaving in and out of rush hour traffic, filled with road-ragers and slowpokes. Oh, and somewhere along the way, you swing through the Taco Bell drive-through and grab a burrito since you haven't eaten since breakfast. Another crazy day in paradise.

And yet after it all, you suddenly find yourself pulling in your driveway. You realize that in all the insanity, you nearly forgot where you were going. You never even consciously concentrated on driving home.

Isn't it amazing that we can do that? We can drive 30 miles across town, have all kinds of distractions, and never once have to think about stopping at this street or turning on that highway.

It all happens automatically; it's second nature, subconscious activity. That's the beauty of it. You don't have to consciously think about driving home from work. You can instead concentrate on dealing with the phone calls—and one crisis after another—and still manage to pull into your driveway.

That's what happens when something in your brain becomes second nature. Once you consciously program the directions from your office to your home and make the trip a few times, your subconscious mind will eventually take over and make the trip without your having to think about it.

Now, consider this question: Could you drive to that same house without thinking about the directions the *first* time you ever drove there? You probably needed a map, GPS, or someone to give you step-by-step instructions on how to get there. Yet after making a few trips, you can complete this goal without a conscious thought. So it follows that you could consciously work on other things, and your subconscious mind, once programmed with the directions, will safely and reliably get you exactly where you want to be.

There is a powerful lesson embodied in this real-life situation, yet it's one that goes unnoticed by the masses. If you can grasp the reality of this experience, you can capture the essence of *The Power of Consistency* and use it to reach virtually any goal you desire.

You can use *The Power of Consistency* to consciously program your sales and business goals—and the activities necessary to reach those goals—into your mind, and then allow your subconscious to take over. From there, your subconscious mind will help you navigate the twists and turns of a successful sales and business career until eventually you arrive at your goals in the same way you navigate traffic to arrive at your home.

Our brain's ability to do this is one of the most powerful forces in our lives. Yet we sometimes have a difficult time understanding this potential of our invisible subconscious mind. We often believe the idiom "out of sight, out of mind." But as we learned from the last chapter, just because we can't *see* what's going on in our heads doesn't mean we can afford to miss their importance. It may be invisible, but it's also invaluable.

Understanding—and effectively using—*The Power of Consistency* to program your subconscious mind is the key to the kingdom for your sales and business results. It is the means by which you can reach virtually any goal you set your subconscious mind to. It is how you can create unlimited wealth and prosperity in your business. Eventually, you'll be able to consciously work on other tasks, such as talking on the phone or solving some pressing problem, while subconsciously making progress toward your business and sales objectives.

What if instead of going from home to work, you replace these two destinations with where you are in life today and where you want to be down the road? What if, for example, you are earning $50,000 a year now and want to earn $150,000?

It is possible to program your subconscious mind to get from one income level to another income level. In the same way you can program your subconscious mind to get you from work to home while you are distracted with other things in life, you can program your subconscious mind to get you from one income level to another while you are distracted with other things in life.

The key is using *The Power of Consistency* to

1. Identify where you want to end up.
2. Identify the specific directions you need to take to reach this goal (in this case, your desired income level).
3. Program those directions into your subconscious mind on an ongoing basis.

Once you program the directions to reach a particular goal into your subconscious mind, it will work on it 24 hours a day, 365 days a year to reach the destination.

And again, it's not mysticism or magic or anything else. It is simply a matter of how your thoughts drive your emotions, which drive your actions, which drive your results. It's all about using *The Power of Consistency* to reprogram your thoughts—in other words, what's in your box.

Consider for a moment how amazing the human body is. Think about your eyes, arms, legs, ears, and nose, and how your heart pumps and your lungs expand and contract all in perfect unison. It's truly a miraculous organism. Everything serves a purpose. It's a very efficient machine. There is no wasted anything.

Now think about this: You have the ability to see amazing things in your mind's eye. You can dream things that haven't happened yet and see those dreams in your mind. You can close your eyes and visualize a house that's not yet built, a relationship that hasn't yet developed, or an income or a business that hasn't yet grown.

Even though these things don't yet exist, you can see every detail if you choose to concentrate on them.

Now here's the thing. If you accept that the human body is amazing and that everything about it serves a purpose, consider this: Either our mind's ability to see wonderful things before they are created serves a purpose—like every other part of our body—or it doesn't. It's either there for a reason, or it's just there to torment us with visions and dreams of things we'll never have.

Which do you suppose it is?

I believe our mind's ability to see amazing things *before* they happen serves a function for us—just like our eyes, heart, lungs, and everything other organ do. I believe that we have the ability to close our eyes and dream because it's the first step toward creating it in our lives.

As Dr. Stephen R. Covey said in *The 7 Habits of Highly Effective People*, "All things are created twice"—once inside the box and once outside the box.

Remember, we are talking about a phenomenon that you've experienced a thousand times before when driving home from work. We are simply going to focus that energy a little more directly. There is nothing here you haven't experienced before; we are just going to take it to another level.

The bottom line is that you have the ability to close your eyes and dream—and therefore, the ability to take the first step toward leveraging *The Power of Consistency* and building the sales and business income you deserve.

The key to reaching this goal is to ingrain the directions to where you want to go into your mind until they become second nature, part of the subconscious mind. Once you do that, you can go through the course of your life confident that you are moving closer to the dream every day, automatically making the twists and turns you need to get there.

Your Reticular Activating System

The reason that this can happen is due to a little part of your brain that is constantly noticing and identifying the resources and opportunities you need to reach your dream. This little part is called the reticular activating system (RAS), and it's the central reason that your results in life can never exceed your expectations. If you want to change your life or create something better, you have to make sure the RAS is on board with your new program.

The RAS is critical to your survival. It helps you notice threats to your well-being so that you can take appropriate actions to protect yourself. It also helps you become aware of opportunities that are relevant to reaching your dreams.

You can think of the RAS as a kind of net that filters out things that are irrelevant to you and lets in the things that are relevant to you. And as we already know, two people can see the same thing and note something very different about it. In general, we tend to notice what has meaning and significance to us.

For example, let's say that we're watching a surfer hit the waves. You may notice right away that he is wearing yellow shorts, whereas I may be oblivious to this detail. They just don't mean anything to me, whereas they reminded you of your father's favorite color. The shorts were *relevant* to you, so you noticed them. They got caught up in your RAS net. But they weren't caught in mine.

There are millions of things you could notice—sights, sounds, movements, smells—at any given moment in your life. Because your conscious mind cannot possibly process all of them at the same time, your RAS prompts you to pay attention to what's relevant and ignore what isn't.

Suppose you are walking down a beautiful trail. You look upon the serene beauty of the mountains, the streams, and the wildlife. You inhale the wildflowers' sweet fragrance and hear the symphony of birds. Your RAS is taking it all in, noticing all the beauty and serenity and putting you completely at peace.

At that moment, a huge mountain lion leaps from a ledge above you and you are face to face with an animal that could kill you with one swat of its paw.

Are you still noticing the beautiful scenery? Do you still smell the flowers? Probably not. The only thing you notice— and care about—is figuring out how to escape.

That is your RAS at work. When the beauty and serenity of the mountains were relevant to you, you noticed them. But when the mountain lion threatened you, the scenery quickly became irrelevant and you noticed the only thing that mattered: getting out of there. Once you realized that you were in danger, your RAS filtered everything else out since those details didn't matter anymore.

Imagine eating a huge meal and being so stuffed that you can barely breathe. Do you think it's possible that in that state you could drive down the main street of your town and go right past every fast-food joint without even noticing them? You bet.

That, again, is your RAS at work. When you don't need food any longer, it filters out the restaurants, deeming them irrelevant. Think about driving down that same street when you are starving. You'll notice every burger and chicken joint on the block, since food is now relevant.

The same is true with auditory cues. Have you ever been in an airport with announcements coming over the public address (PA) system? Name after name is broadcast, but you hear nothing but white noise. What do you suppose your RAS would do if *your name* was announced over the PA system? Would you notice it? Of course you would, because your name is relevant to you.

I've always been a news and politics junkie. Even during the years I was in prison, I can remember watching the *MacNeil/Lehrer NewsHour* on PBS. I also remember turning the channel right past news stories on taxes and our national debt, because at the time those issues had no significance to me. I was broke and in prison. Problems with debt and taxes were completely irrelevant to my life at that time, so my RAS filtered it out.

I never skip over stories on those topics today, however, because they're now very relevant to my life and business. And right on cue, my RAS makes sure I don't miss that information.

The RAS's job of filtering out of irrelevant information and capturing relevant information has *enormous* implications for your ability to create wealth in sales and business.

Imagine your income expectation is a middle income of $50,000 a year. During your childhood, your family and the neighbors were middle-income families, as was everyone you knew in your socioeconomic circle. As a result, middle income is in your box—and that's pretty much what you expect to make.

Then suppose a million-dollar opportunity crossed your career path. Do you think your RAS might be inclined to filter out that opportunity as irrelevant? Of course it could. In fact, it's very likely that you'll miss big opportunities if your subconscious perceives them as irrelevant to your life and career.

Therefore, if you want to notice those incredible opportunities, you have to make sure that they're in your box, thereby keeping your RAS from labeling them as irrelevant. As we work through this first step, you will have the opportunity to identify what you want in your career and to put those things in your box.

In addition to dismissing irrelevant information, your RAS can often reject information that you disagree with or that challenges what you believe. In essence, your RAS will take in information that reinforces your beliefs and will ignore anything that challenges them.

Suppose, for example, you believe that price is the most important factor prospects weigh when making a purchasing decision. Price sensitivity is in your box. If that's your basic belief and attitude, you will notice every instance where price is an issue, and those are likely the experiences you remember and talk about. You essentially notice the events that reinforce your basic belief system.

But what about the times your prospects don't buy on price? Do you remember those instances, or do you write them off as anomalies or refer to them as the occasional "lay-down" who buys without any objections or price resistance? You are likely to remember the events that reinforce your basic views and expectations.

The reality is that both sides of everything are out there. The "economy sucks" is out there, and the "economy is good" is out there. "Customers buy on price" is out there, and "customers buy on value" is out there. The question is which one do you notice? Which one reinforces your expectations and beliefs? Either way, you will prove yourself right.

In other words, your RAS notices information that proves you right and discounts any that proves you wrong. This is why you are pretty much right 100 percent of the time! Your RAS essentially goes out into the world and accumulates all the information that reinforces what you already believe, which is why your career and business are self-fulfilling prophecies.

Ask yourself how often you are surprised by what happens in your sales and business career. Don't prospects pretty much behave the way you expect them to? Don't you lose the sales you expect to lose and win the ones you expect to win?

The answer is likely yes, because expectations always drive your results. If you want to change your results, you have to change your expectations.

The RAS is a powerful part of your life. It has the potential to create amazing things, but it's also a double-edged sword in its ability to destroy potential and opportunity. Like so many other invisible forces in life, we don't completely understand it, and therefore we often discount its importance in helping create the sales and business results we desire.

Once you understand the RAS's two basic functions—to dismiss irrelevant information and notice relevant information and to reinforce what you already believe—then things get really interesting.

Your box holds your basic belief system about business and wealth, along with any thoughts and expectations about your professional success. Everything you believe—as well as the things you expect to happen—are all right there. And we know that whatever is in your box will eventually be proved right.

The problem is that the RAS will find information to prove you right—*even if you are wrong*.

You see, the RAS is a filter, but it doesn't *have* a filter. It reinforces whatever you already believe, for better or for worse. It doesn't discriminate against things that are inaccurate reflections of reality. Remember, if you think something is true, it's true—even if it's not true.

In that way, your RAS will prove you right, even if you're wrong.

If you think you *can* prosper in a bad economy, you will notice ways that you can prosper, such as when you earn a prospect's trust and business by focusing on value, quality, and service. If you think you *cannot* prosper in a bad economy, you will notice the things that prove you right, such as the times when a prospect works you over and gives you the order only after you drop your price. Again, both scenarios are out there, the issue is, what do you notice?

That's why two completely reasonable people can see the same situation so differently. Both are adamant and passionate about their views. They can't believe the other person can't see what is so obvious to them. Each person has different junk in the trunk, and each person's RAS is programmed to prove him or her right—even when wrong!

This is where the RAS can completely take over your life, for better or for worse, because it's going to prove your beliefs right.

Suppose you work in sales, and you're feeling lately like the economy sucks. You assume that the only way you can sell your products in this down economy is to lower your prices. Do you think that your RAS might go out into the world and notice the information that proves you right? Of course it will. You will notice with keen sensitivity anytime a prospect objects to price, which will drive your overall expectations.

Even if a customer buys from you *without* asking for a discount, you will dismiss it as an anomaly, because that does not comport with your basic view of customers. In fact, your RAS will have you remembering the customer who demanded a discount for weeks, while instantly forgetting the customer who didn't.

The good news is that this reality works in the opposite direction too. A person with very positive beliefs and expectations will almost instantly forget a negative situation that does not reinforce his or her mindset and remember a positive situation that does. If you believe that there are still customers out there who are willing to pay for superior service and quality despite the tough economy, you're likely to encounter information that proves you right. Moreover, you will remember the experiences that reinforce your beliefs and expectations and dismiss as anomalies experiences that do not.

The reality is that both a bad and a good economy—and both good customers and bad customers—are out there. Which ones will you notice and use to define your basic expectations?

How you program your RAS over the long term will determine your answer to this question.

That's why your sales results will never exceed your sales expectations. Your RAS is going to prove your expectations right every time.

The unfortunate news is that many of us have very limiting expectations in our box. And once they are in there, they drastically limit what we can achieve and create. Without a process to get the bad stuff out and replace it with unlimited expectations, we frequently find ourselves stuck. So when you consider that we all have some negative stuff in our trunk—and that our RAS will notice things to continue to prove them accurate—it's easy to see how a less-than-fulfilling sales and business career can perpetuate itself. We get junk in our trunks, it comes true (and we notice and remember it), and we grow more pessimistic about life, thereby putting more junk in the trunk that the RAS again proves right.

It's a vicious cycle.

When I was a kid, my dad used to say, "Rich people are crooks. No one becomes rich without screwing a few folks along the way." That was something put in his box somewhere along the way, and something that he then put it into my box. Thus, I grew up being very suspicious of successful, wealthy people. I'd see someone with a nice car, big home, or successful company, and I'd find myself saying, "Wonder who they screwed?"

It never occurred to me that honest, hardworking people build successful companies and live in beautiful homes. I always thought they spent their time screwing people. That's what was in my box.

It therefore doesn't come as much of a surprise to me, looking back over my life, that when I wanted nice things, I didn't see the problem with breaking the law to get them. After all, rich people are crooks, and if I needed to break the rules to get ahead, so be it. I believed that's how successful people became successful. Obviously, my father was in no way responsible for the destructive and criminal lifestyle I chose. My father was a hardworking, career military man who looked with disdain at the life I led.

I'm just saying that you can occasionally put something in other people's boxes that they might bring to fruition. Not because they believe it's right, but because the RAS is so powerful at making thoughts seem accurate.

For instance, have you ever known a kid who was told, "You'll never amount to anything" or "You're stupid"? How many times have you seen that prophecy come true?

Once we get things in our heads we tend to prove them right—for better or for worse. The key to creating wealth in sales and business is figuring out what's in your box, getting the bad stuff out, putting good stuff in, and letting your RAS prove you right in a good way. Once you understand how your RAS works, it's easy to see the role it plays in the quality and circumstances of your sales and business career.

So unless you want to miss out on amazing opportunities, you'd better make sure your mind is programmed to think *anything is possible*. Otherwise, the opportunity of a lifetime can go right past you.

Talk to any really successful person you know, and that person will tell you that wealth, prosperity, and success are very often the intersection of timing and opportunity. Of course, working hard and capitalizing on the opportunity are necessary, but finding the opportunity at the right time is critical.

I have seen this countless times in my life and business. As I look back over the key opportunities I've had, I know it's impossible to ignore how I stumbled into the right opportunity at the right time. I wish I could tell you I single-handedly created my companies from sheer genius, but the truth is, most of my success has resulted from timing and opportunity.

Did I capitalize on the opportunities? Absolutely. *But first I had to notice them.* More accurately, my RAS first had to notice them and perceive them as relevant to my life. Fortunately, I harness *The Power of Consistency* to program wealth and prosperity into my subconscious, so I did not miss the opportunities to make those dreams a reality.

The first company I started in 2004 was a heating and air-conditioning company—a business that exploded over the first few years. In our first year, we generated $2 million in sales; we generated $3.5 million in our second year and $7 million in our third year—making a total of more than $20 million in sales in our first 60 months. In 2009, *Inc.* magazine recognized our company as one of the fastest-growing privately held companies in America.

Now it might be tempting for me to tell you this success proves how brilliant I am, but the reality is that it was timing and opportunity. The market was right. The right people were available. I just caught the wave.

The more success I have in life, the more I am convinced that it's all about timing and opportunity—being in the right place at the right time. The key is *noticing* the opportunity at the right time and perceiving it as relevant to your life, which means making sure your RAS is programmed to do so.

If I had walked out of prison merely expecting to get some kind of a job, and maybe—if I was lucky—a small apartment, I would have missed the amazing opportunity to build my first company from scratch. I would have been oblivious to the myriad of things that had to fall in place to make it all happen. My RAS would have filtered all those little things out as being irrelevant.

If my expectation had been to get a job, I would have seen my sales success as "mission accomplished." I would have reached my goal of getting a job and stopped right there.

But because I had spent years conditioning my subconscious with beliefs and expectations that I would be a successful entrepreneur, I looked beyond my sales success to see the potential for success as an entrepreneur in the heating and air-conditioning industry. I saw the business opportunity in an industry that was fractured and disorganized because my RAS was searching for a business opportunity. Had I been searching for a sales job, that's all I would have found.

Furthermore, because I had also programmed my RAS to be on the lookout for speaking and sales training opportunities within my industry, I noticed several opportunities for me to do that too. As a result, I am now recognized as one on the nation's foremost experts on the "residential kitchen-table sales process." I don't say that to impress you. I say it to impress upon you the power of programming your RAS to be on the lookout for new opportunities to create wealth and prosperity.

It's like that old joke about always finding your car keys in the last place you look. Once you find what you're looking for, it's human nature to stop looking. You've got to program your RAS to be on the lookout for unlimited success and prosperity in your sales and business career, because once you reach your goal, your RAS will stop looking for new opportunities unless you give it something else to look for. Maybe instead of just looking for your keys, you might consider also looking for a new car to put them in . . . and then a new garage to park the new car in.

I was able to begin living a life of happiness and success because I took a crucial first step: Identifying exactly what I wanted and programming it into to my subconscious mind like the route from my office to my home. Once you do that, your RAS won't be able to filter out new opportunities as irrelevant. If you expect amazing things in your life, your RAS will prove you right.

As you work through the remainder of this book, you will learn the step-by-step process for creating your prosperity plan and how to implement that plan on a consistent basis. That's really where the rubber meets the road: You have to *do* what you outline in your plan. I am going to teach you a simple process that will keep you on track to achieving your dreams.

This process requires that you take a look inside your box, get the bad stuff out, and replace it with a *ton* of good stuff. This will allow you to alter your expectation of what's possible for you. Once you change your thoughts, your emotions will follow—and as you know, actions and results will be right on their heels.

As you begin making progress toward your dreams, you will also be programming your subconscious mind to expect the amazing things you outline in your prosperity plan. You will map out the directions to prosperity, and the journey will eventually become second nature. Moreover, you will establish expectations that your RAS will facilitate. You will begin to notice opportunities that you would have previously missed. With these new opportunities firmly in focus—and the expectation that you will create wealth, happiness, and peace of mind in your life and business—the career and business of your dreams will begin to take shape. You deserve wealth and prosperity, and the process we are going to work through will help you create them.

Once you complete the process and begin implementing the plan, you will notice an immediate shift in your emotions, growing confidence, and more lofty goals and expectations.

You'll begin to expect better things, and you'll begin to believe that you can achieve any level of success and prosperity in your life and business.

Perhaps most important, you will find yourself strengthened and empowered to do the *little things* you need to do on a consistent basis to create new levels of prosperity and success in your sales career.

The process of changing what's in your box is critical. To do so, we will use the upside of FEAR process:

*F*ocus
*E*motional commitment
*A*ction
*R*esponsibility

I mentioned earlier in this book how fear governed my life, thereby compelling me to actually *attract* the things I feared into it. That was the downside of fear.

The upside of FEAR process is the process of getting your mind right and programming it for wealth, happiness, and peace of mind in your life and business. Once it's programmed deep in your subconscious mind, you will find your way there—just like you find your way home from work without consciously thinking about it.

I vividly remember the moment I realized how powerful the subconscious conditioning process is. It took place long before any external changes in my life. The transformation started inside as I began to notice a powerful emotional shift.

It was only a few days after I began the process of reviewing my prosperity plan during what I call a daily quiet-time ritual. I was walking laps within the perimeter of the cell house, as I often did for exercise, when suddenly I was overcome with a powerful sense of hopefulness and confidence that my life was about to drastically change.

Out of nowhere—despite facing years more in prison and a very bleak future—I began to feel a sense of excitement and enthusiasm. After just a few days of embracing more positive, empowering, and hopeful thoughts, my underlying emotions began to change.

As soon as I began consistently telling myself I was going to become a wealthy, successful person, I began to *feel* like a winner, instead of feeling like a loser. I was overwhelmed with the belief that great things were going to happen in my life. I changed my thoughts by changing the contents of my box, and by doing so, I changed the way I felt. Eventually those new emotions triggered different actions, which of course eventually led to different results. Next thing you know, *everything* had changed—for the better.

I truly believe that you will have a similar experience. Obviously, everyone's dreams are different. But whatever yours are, you will begin to experience powerful emotions as you articulate those dreams in a clear concise fashion. As you review them during your daily quiet-time ritual, you will find yourself acting in a manner consistent with the things you want in life and business. And as you do this, you will find yourself creating the results that you want and deserve.

You will place the income and career you desire into your box, piece by piece, dream by dream. Then you will begin pulling the new results out of your box—step by step, moment by moment, and day by day.

You will find it easier to do the things you already know you should be doing. You will find your willpower and confidence to stay on track with your dreams strengthened.

And even before you and others see the physical manifestations of your thoughts in your income and career, you will experience new emotions that lead to a more fulfilling and rewarding life. You'll start feeling better, more confident, and more hopeful.

As you work through *The Power of Consistency*, you will outline your prosperity plan, and you will begin to see amazing things happen.

CHAPTER THREE

Understanding the Power of Focus and Your Subconscious Mind

That's been one of my mantras—focus and simplicity. Simple can be harder than complex: You have to work hard to get your thinking clean to make it simple. But it's worth it in the end because once you get there, you can move mountains.

—Steve Jobs

Imagine that you had a goal and decided to focus *solely* on achieving that one thing—to the exclusion of anything and everything else.

Let's say, for the sake of example, that this one thing was building a house.

Building that house was the only thing you thought about. The only books you read were books on how to build that house. The only conversations you would have were conversations about building that house. Every night when you slept, you dreamt of only that house.

You were consumed with this task to the point of obsession. Every moment of your life was devoted to building that house or figuring out how to get the money and materials you need to do so.

With that level of commitment, what are the chances you would eventually achieve your dream of creating that house?

I'd say pretty good. How could you not achieve something you were so laser-focused on?

Now imagine that you devote that level of focus to building your sales and business income. Imagine that degree of intensity every morning as you begin your day and having such concentrated focus on every sales call with every prospect.

What do you suppose that level of focus would do for your sales productivity? Would your business benefit from that kind of intense concentration? You would very likely write more business and earn a better income, because that level of focus would ensure your status as a top producer.

It sounds like a promising scenario, right? But there is a problem—a big problem: It's impossible to stay *that* obsessively focused on one thing for more than a short time.

Everyone has countless responsibilities in life in addition to building a career and running a business. You have a family that consumes time and energy. You have bills to pay. You have friends who need you and with whom you want to spend time. You have a million distractions in your life that prevent you from focusing on one thing to the exclusion of everything else.

If you were to focus—solely and obsessively—on building that house, there is a pretty good chance you would live in it alone when it was finished. Your friends and family would feel alienated, because, as most of us know, obsessing on one single thing all the time is not a very healthy way to live. Your family and friends wouldn't think much of you. You wouldn't be very happy, even when you created your dream.

The same goes for your sales and business career. That level of obsessive focus would guarantee a successful business—but you'd probably be enjoying it all alone.

So there is a catch-22. It's very exciting, on one hand, to know that you could achieve or have anything you want in life if you could just focus on that one thing exclusively. On the other hand, that's basically impossible for anyone to do. We all have countless things, people, and activities that need our attention and a variety of distractions that consume our time and energy—and prevent us from focusing *exclusively* on making our dreams a reality.

When the conscious mind *is* laser-focused, it's a powerful tool for processing information, solving problems, and transforming thoughts into reality. Unfortunately, for the reasons previously cited, we can't typically focus on *one thing* and nothing else. But the truth is most of us only truly excel when we focus on one thing at a time.

Think about a time where you accomplished something that made you feel like a rock star. Maybe you completed a kick-ass project for work or school, achieved a physical feat you'd been working toward, or built something amazing. Did you stumble into that success accidentally, or was it the product of focus and concentration?

Take a moment and really think about your accomplishment. How did you get started? What specific steps did you take to reach your goal? What level of commitment did it take? How bad did you want it? Odds are your creation was no accident.

So how do you reconcile these competing realities? You want to focus on creating the income and career of your dreams, but you have other responsibilities that consume your time and energy. You have countless distractions that prevent you from achieving the things you want to achieve.

The answer to this conundrum lies in the subconscious part of your brain—in changing what's in your subconscious mind so that you can move toward achieving your dreams while your conscious mind juggles all of life's everyday distractions. The answer lies in changing the contents of your box.

Although your conscious mind is at its best when focusing on one thing at a time, the subconscious mind is a brilliant multitasker. It can process multiple streams of information, solve numerous problems, and transform several thoughts into reality on a fairly predictable basis.

In fact, the *conscious* mind's chief limitation—its inability to focus on multiple things at one time—is the *subconscious* mind's primary strength.

Once you've programmed a destination into your subconscious mind, you can move consistently toward it, despite the distractions that consume your conscious mind. It works when you are driving home from work and for anything else you program into the subconscious.

Stop for a moment and think about an outcome you can reach without a conscious focus. Earlier I used the example of driving home from work without the need for conscious focus, but what other examples can you come up with? How about cooking or making a sandwich? Do you have to consciously focus on each layer of ham or spreading the mayo? Probably not.

I have seen people who love to knit weave their way to a beautiful scarf while carrying on a conversation the entire time. Think about something you enjoy doing, and you can probably do it without conscious thought once it becomes second nature.

The point is that you can program the steps to accomplish something into your subconscious mind and then reach your desired outcome without having to consciously focus your attention.

This same process can—and *will*—work for your income and sales career if you program the results you want and deserve. Once your goals regarding this area of your life are programmed into your subconscious mind, your RAS will process the information, opportunities, and actions you need to get there.

If you don't think that this is possible, then you may have to concede that your ability to see your dreams in your mind's eye is there only to torment you with visions of things you can never have. If you believe the components of your body all serve a vital purpose, it makes sense that your ability to dream new realities does so as well.

Think about how you can do multiple things at the same time once they have become second nature in your subconscious mind. Think about the drive from your office to your home. Not only can you do that without consciously thinking about it, but you could also carry on a conversation, eat a cheeseburger, and listen to the radio—all at the same time and all without crashing your car. (By the way, although many of us can relate to the driving example, it remains imperative to remain aware of driving conditions and refrain from dangerous activities such as texting while driving. This example does not imply that you can drive home while texting or putting on makeup any more than you could drive home with your eyes closed. Just saying.)

That's what happens when something becomes second nature. You don't have to think about what to do while you're doing it.

This is a critically important point: When something is programmed into your subconscious, you can make progress toward your destination even while you are thinking about and doing something completely unrelated.

This is the key to *The Power of Consistency*. The secret to achieving incredible levels of wealth, happiness, and prosperity in your sales and business career is taking consistent action toward those dreams. And the way to ensure you are taking consistent action toward your dreams is to make that action part of your subconscious thoughts—to make it second nature.

When you do this, you will find yourself consistently taking steps toward your goals, regardless of how distracted you are by other responsibilities that consume your time and energy. And just in the way you find yourself pulling in your driveway after a long day at work, you will eventually find yourself experiencing your dreams in a very real way. The key is keeping your subconscious mind focused on them.

Once you have programmed your prosperity plan into your subconscious mind, your reticular activating system (RAS) will also ensure that you do not miss out on the timing and opportunity you need to make your plans become a reality. In fact, your RAS will work 24 hours a day, 365 days a year to uncover those opportunities and figure out exactly what resources it needs to get you where you want to go.

Although this might all sound new to you, there have doubtlessly been instances throughout your life where you have fully experienced the power of the RAS and subconscious thoughts. For example, think about a time when you've suddenly realized the solution to a problem you had previously been unable to solve. You begin consciously contemplating a solution, and your subconscious mind continues to work on it long after your conscious mind has moved on to something else. Next thing you know, you awaken in the middle of the night with the solution to your problem. Eventually the solution reveals itself as the RAS continues to notice and filter information relevant to the problem.

Think about a time when you suddenly recalled the name of a movie, an actor, or a song that you had earlier been unable to remember. You move on with your day, but your RAS continues to process information until suddenly it finds the answer and brings it to your consciousness. That is what the RAS does. Once you give it instructions or a destination, it will work non-stop, without consuming your conscious attention, to figure out how to get there.

This is precisely why focusing on achieving your income and sales goal is vital to accomplishing it. The key is programming your subconscious mind to stay focused on achieving your dreams even when your conscious mind gets distracted.

If you stay obsessively focused on something, you will eventually achieve it. That's the power of focus. You may have discovered the power of focus as a kid when you learned how to enhance the sun's energy with a magnifying glass. (For anyone who's never done this, it's pretty cool!) You discovered that you were able to transform the sun's warmth into a weapon by focusing its energy through the magnifying glass. You could light leaves on fire or carve your name into a piece of wood. You can take the sun's already intense energy and use the magnifying glass to multiply it.

The same thing is true in regard to the incredible power of your brain. It is intensely powerful to begin with, and by using the power of focus, you can actually magnify that intensity and achieve anything. You can create unimaginable levels of wealth and prosperity. There are no limits to what you can do if you are willing to focus your subconscious mind's energy on a specific objective.

As we begin the upside of FEAR process in the next chapter, you will learn exactly how to focus on your personal and professional dreams and then use a simple process to add the instructions to reach those dreams to your box, programming them into your subconscious mind. Once you have finished this process, simply go about your conscious, daily activities and allow your RAS to get to work. You will find yourself effort-lessly doing the things you need to do to reach your dreams. And before you know it, without a conscious thought, you will find yourself at your dream destination in the same way you find yourself in your driveway after work.

Understand that it is critical to become focused on *exactly* what you want in life and business and then program those things into your subconscious mind. It's not good enough to have a *general* idea of your life goals; you must know precisely where you want to end and what it looks—and feels—like to be there.

Think back again to the example of driving from work to home. Can you say you've reached your goal if you just end up in the right neighborhood, or is it necessary to get precisely in your driveway?

Obviously, it is the latter. Imagine walking into your neigh-bor's house and trying to explain why you've parked your car in his or her driveway! In other words, close enough isn't good enough. You must get *there*. And once your subconscious mind is programmed to reach your dreams, your RAS will not filter out new business or income opportunities as being irrelevant. You'll know that anything is possible, and you'll come to expect better things for yourself *and* for those around you.

Your expectations will soar. You will demand more from yourself and will live life knowing that you are capable of achieving anything you set your mind to.

The key to all of this is *consistency*—that is, doing the little things you know you need to do over and over again. Once you complete the FEAR process and program your subconscious mind for your amazing new sales career, you will experience *The Power of Consistency* as you move toward your dreams. You will learn the exact process of thinking the right things and doing the right things. And let's face it, if you are *thinking* the right things and *doing* the right things, you can only *create* the right results. After all, you can't focus on building a motorcycle and accidentally bake a cake, right?

You will also learn the importance of a daily quiet-time ritual. This process will give you the strength you require to do the things necessary to create wealth, happiness, and prosperity. You will find a sense of peace and become confident that you are destined to create your dreams by staying focused and consistently moving toward them.

Then, each degree of confidence you attain will foster deeper levels of confidence. As your confidence grows, you will find yourself inspired and able to complete the small daily tasks that will keep you moving forward toward your dreams. Instead of finding yourself frustrated by falling short, you will find yourself empowered to do more. Whether that little thing is one more cold call or closing one more deal, you will have the power and confidence to create anything you set your mind to.

It doesn't matter if you have fallen short before, or if you have struggled for years. It doesn't matter if you made bad choices and created problems in your life. It doesn't matter if you have tried to change before and failed.

Today is a new day. The process I am going to walk you through—that we will undergo together—can change everything, *if* you are willing to do the work. It's nothing that's extremely difficult or demanding, since the things you need to do are fairly simple and easy. Of course, it's always simpler and easier not to do them.

Remember the conundrum of human nature: *knowing exactly what you need to do to increase your sales and grow your income but not doing it on a consistent basis.*

This is your time to rise up, take control of your destiny, and build the life of your dreams. It can feel overwhelming, and it may seem like a long shot, but you must do it anyway. I know you've tried before and fallen short, but you must get back up and do it again.

I know exactly how you feel. I've been there. I wrote the book on falling down and getting back up (literally). I understand what you are going through. I was the *king* of mistakes and bad choices.

But you can do this. Just stick with it step by step, little by little making progress toward the end goal. You can and *will* take consistent action toward achieving your income and sales potential.

Whatever your dreams are, you are going to have the plan and the strength to take consistent action to create amazing things in your life and business.

Stay focused. Never surrender. Never compromise. Your dreams are closer than you realize. Now let's get started on going after them.

CHAPTER FOUR

Step 1: Focus

You can't depend on your eyes when your imagination is out of focus.

—Mark Twain

If you want to create powerful results in sales and business, it's not enough to be efficient; you must be *effective*. And you do this by focusing on the right things. The vast majority of poor performance that I see in sales and business professionals does not stem from lack of ability, skill, or training. It is the direct result of people's tendency to focus on the wrong things.

Many of us go through life just "thinking" on autopilot. We are operating out of our subconscious programming in the way we drive home from work without consciously thinking about where we are going. In this section, we will begin to turn that inclination around by "thinking about what we are thinking about." As you begin to understand how powerful your thoughts are in relation to your sales and business success, you'll appreciate how important it is to spend a little time thinking about the things you think about.

As the great philosopher Socrates said, "An unexamined life is not worth living." Our job in this section of the book is to examine what's currently in your box—and whether it should stay or go. Much of what's in there has been there since childhood, so once you become an adult, it's your choice to hoard all the contents and wallow in it or clear out the junk and organize what remains.

Step 1 in the Upside of the FEAR process is getting *focused* on the right things—specifically, on what you want to achieve in your sales and business career. This process requires that you identify your ultimate destination, determine a few simple steps that will get you there, and recognize any limiting beliefs that may undermine your ability to get there. We also need to ensure that we are focusing on the right things in sales and business.

To truly create a prosperity mindset that's capable of generating powerful sales and business results, we must *think about
what we think about*—and we must make sure we are thinking
about the right things.

This process will take you beyond your sales and business career
goals and help you identify what you want in the larger scope of
life. Expanding our scope like this is necessary, because our moti-
vation to succeed in business often comes from more deeply held
desires pertaining to our life as a whole—that is, to provide for our
families or help others through the work that we do.

In this chapter you will consider:

- What you want
- What you want to *become*
- What you want to *contribute*
- What you need to do to accomplish these things
- What limiting beliefs may be holding you back in life and
  business

The information you unearth as you work through the first
four of these areas will form the basis for creating your prosperity plan. The fifth component is designed to help you identify
deeply held limiting beliefs that may be undermining your success in life. Once you identify these, you will be able to create
new thoughts and beliefs that counteract their negative, limiting
effects on your life.

Don't worry about organizing the information as you
undergo this process, because the next step involves putting
it all together in a cohesive prosperity plan. The point of this
section is simply to let your imagination flow. This phase is
about creativity. It's about dreaming big.

Keep the following in mind as you contemplate the life
and business of your dreams: You don't have to be practical.

Remember, we have an imagination for a reason, so let it run wild. We weren't given the ability to dream amazing dreams only so we could be tormented by visions of things we can never have. We must elevate our expectations through the use of creative thought, and imagining a better life is the first step in achieving this vision.

When I think back to the first time I outlined my prosperity plan—while sitting in my cell—I am surprised by the audacity of my dreams. I think about the nature and circumstances of my life and contrast that with the dreams I began to imagine. If I had stuck with reasonable and practical expectations, I likely would have dreamed only of finding a job and staying out of jail. But I wanted more than that—a lot more. I wanted to accomplish huge things in my life. I wanted more than mediocrity. I wanted to create an exceptional life.

Contrast what I wanted and wrote down with where I actually was in my life at that time:

- I wanted to be an awesome father to my son despite the fact I had abandoned him and was facing seven more years in prison.
- I wanted to have an education despite having dropped out of high school in the ninth grade.
- I wanted to own a beautiful mountain home despite having never owned a home in my life.
- I wanted to become a successful businessman, speaker, and writer despite never having done any of those things and having no reason to believe that I could do any of them.
- I wanted to write a book on the beaches of Maui despite having no reason to believe I could write a book and barely even knowing where Maui was on a map.
- I wanted to be wealthy despite earning only prison wages of a few dollars per month.
- I wanted to find an amazing wife, despite having failed in all my previous relationships.

- I wanted to become a man of character, honor, and integrity despite being a three-time convicted felon and having spent my entire life lying, cheating, and stealing.

My expectations for a new life were *anything* but reasonable. Anyone sitting with me in my cell hearing my dreams would have called me a madman. But dreaming big is an important part of the process.

Remember, your results in life will never exceed your expectations, and your expectations will never exceed your imagination. That's precisely why you must allow yourself to dream big. Don't limit yourself with being reasonable or practical. As the late Dr. Stephen R. Covey famously advised, we don't have to live out of our pasts. We can live out of our imaginations.

As you work through the first step of this process, you are going to begin putting new things in your box that you can later pull out. Your thoughts are the contents of your box. As you put the life and business of your dreams in your box, you will also examine the negative, limiting beliefs that may already be in there.

Take a sheet of paper and start making notes as we work through this. Don't try to complete it in a hurry. After you read a section, stop and think about what you would like to accomplish and make notes. Again, we will organize your notes in the next step.

We will begin this discussion by talking about what you want in life. Although these might not be the most important things we discuss, I find that most people can quickly identify these things, so it's a good place to begin outlining your prosperity plan.

We will consider increasingly important factors of your life as we walk through this exercise.

What You Want in Life and Business

The most important thing here is to be as specific and precise as possible about each area of your life. As you contemplate each area, jot down whatever comes to mind.

Think, for instance, about your income and discern *exactly* what level of financial security you want. How much do you want to earn annually or over the course of your career? Think about how you will quantify this figure. What does financial success look like in your mind?

Maybe it's a certain amount of wealth at retirement age. Maybe you define it in terms of ensuring a college education for your children or moving into a certain type of home. The bottom line is that you must define financial success according to how it feels and looks to you—including as many specific details as possible.

Take some time to let your mind explore the possibilities. The key is to allow your creativity to take over and let your imagination flow freely. And again, *be precise*. If you define financial success by your financial condition at retirement, choose a specific age and amount of wealth for retirement. If you define success by being able to provide a college education for your children, figure out exactly how much money you'd need for this; you might even try to picture them at a particular school. If your goal is to own a certain type of house, envision your dream home's details and characteristics.

I remember reading the Sunday newspaper a year or so ago and coming across an ad for an exotic sports car—the one that had been my dream car when I was kid. I cut out the picture of the car, held it up, and declared, "This is my next car!" I then put the picture on our refrigerator.

Over the next few months, I would look at the picture on the refrigerator and slowly started to think, "Wow! Wouldn't that be something? Imagine having the car I fantasized about as a kid!"

Eventually I added the car to my prosperity plan. Less than a year later, I owned that exact car. Not one similar to it, but the *exact* model car I had cut out of the paper and put on the fridge. Because I was dreaming big and being specific—and giving myself a daily reminder of my goal—I was able to achieve it.

If your dream is to improve your sales performance and grow your business, consider what success will look like in your career. Is it defined by market share or achieving certain levels of revenue or profitability? Maybe you define it by opening a certain number of branches or serving a certain number of clients. Or maybe success in your business means achieving a specific level of customer satisfaction.

Jot down whatever measurement comes to mind; there is no right or wrong way to define success. The so-called right answer is the one that feels right to you. The key is simply to have some unit of measurement, since this will be useful in helping you get there—and knowing when you've arrived.

And don't assume that conventional units of business performance are the best option. The best way for you to measure success is the one that's significant to you—and about which you can get passionate and excited.

For example, when I started a company in my living room in 2004, I defined success as being the leader in our market, holding the number one market share position. I decided that I would know we were successful when we were pulling more installation permits that any of our competitors. Over the first four years of our business, we pulled more than twice as many permits than our nearest competitor.

I had a specific target that I got excited and passionate about. This target drove and motivated me to keep pressing forward during challenging times.

The key to success is having a plan and taking consistent action toward that plan. Defining your dreams in a manner that creates excitement, enthusiasm, and passion will work in conjunction with other strategies in this book to get you where you want to be. The more meaningful the dream is to you, the better.

Don't worry about how you are going to reach your income, sales, and other financial goals at this point. The process you are working through is designed to get you to figure out what you need to do on a regular basis. Your job right now is to stay focused on how you want the outcome to look. There will be plenty of time later on to figure out the steps you'll need to take to get there.

Continue working through what you want in life and business. Write down whatever comes to mind, whatever it is—one word, a complete sentence, or even a partial thought. We'll organize these thoughts and words in the next step.

It is crucial that you ferret out the details about what you really and truly want as you contemplate these goals. By going beyond the surface, you may find that your goals are not exactly what you thought they were.

For example, I was once speaking at a live event where I asked audience members to step up to the microphone and outline what they wanted in life and business. A gentleman came forward and stated that he wanted to continue learning through his retirement and document his decades of learning in a book to teach others what he had learned over the course of his life.

"So you want to write a book?" I asked.

"Yes," he responded.

I continued, "Why do you want to write a book?"

"Because there is so much I have learned, and I want to pass that on to future generations."

"So what you really want is to leave a legacy?"

He thought for a moment and said, "Yeah. What I really want is to leave a legacy."

"That's different than writing a book, right?" I inquired. "A book is just one vehicle you could use to leave a legacy."

"I guess so. I never thought about it like that," he concluded.

This interaction illustrates our need to closely examine what we really want in life and business—because sometimes, what we think we want is actually a *vehicle* to get what we really want.

There is a popular marketing example related to this. Consider that millions of half-inch drill bits are sold each year. Knowing this, how many people want half-inch drill bits each year? The initial answer might seem to be "millions." The actual answer is, "None. Millions of people want a half-inch hole." The drill bit is simply the vehicle that millions of people used to get the half-inch hole they really wanted.

The point is this: Think about what you really want in life and make sure what you think you want is not actually a vehicle to get what you really want.

Again, you will be far more inspired to reach your dreams by identifying what really motivates you. If you think you want money—and you discover that what you really want is security for your family—you will undermine your own success by focusing on money.

Take some time now and reflect on what you want—and remember, there's no need to hurry. Get out a sheet of paper, sit back and relax, and get crystal clear on what you want. Once you figure out the specifics, we'll start the process of loading it all into your box.

What You Want to Become in Life and Business

The next phase of the focus step is to identify what you want to become in life and business, which requires that you go a little deeper than you did in identifying what you want. This goes to the heart of what kind of person you want to be, both personally and professionally. It's also about identifying the principles that will be at the core of defining your life and business.

Dr. Covey brilliantly distinguishes the difference between values and principles in *The 7 Habits of Highly Effective People* by explaining it in the following way: Principles are universal truths. They go deeper than values. Criminals share common values, whereas principles are universally accepted by everyone as good and decent.

Identifying what you want to become requires that you clarify the principles that will govern your life and career. You can then put those in your box and condition your subconscious accordingly. Eventually, you will pull them out in the form of daily choices, which ultimately define your quality of life and career.

I had a long row to hoe when I went through the process of outlining what kind of person I wanted to become. I was, after all, a career criminal. Nevertheless I followed the advice outlined in Covey's book to get a clear picture of what I wanted to become.

Consider the following exercise as a way to help you figure this out. Imagine yourself attending the funeral of someone who is beloved by all who know him. As you enter the room, you see the faces of his grieving friends and loved ones. You approach the casket to pay your final respects, and you are startled to see it is you lying in state. This is your funeral.

Think about what you would want each of your friends, family members, and business associates to say as you look around the room. This will give you a very good idea of what is really important to you. And once you figure this out, you'll have a clear guide to govern your actions.

When I first completed this exercise, first outlined by Dr. Covey, I imagined what I would want my son to say at my funeral. Because of my homeless and impoverished state, I assumed my number one priority was making money. However, I realized as I considered what I wanted my son to say that it wasn't really important that he acknowledge my financial condition at the end of the line. Instead, I envisioned him saying something like "Although my dad was a real knucklehead for the first half of his life, when the light went on, he promised me that he would never leave me or lie to me again. And he kept those promises until the day he died."

That exercise clarified for me what kind of father I wanted to become. Once I put being that father into my box, I had a clear standard of what should govern my priorities.

Think about what kind of legacy you will—and want to— leave as you work through this exercise. What will people say about you when you are gone? What would you want them to say? What kind of business owner or manager do you want them to remember you as? What kind of sales professional?

Get clear about what you want to become. Later we'll put that in the box with the things you want—and those will eventually be what you'll pull out of the box.

What You Want to Contribute in Life and Business

Next, begin identifying what you want to contribute in your career. A true sales professional has the opportunity to solve problems for others and improve the quality of others' lives and businesses. As Leo Tolstoy said, "Service is the true meaning of life"—something I have increasingly found to be true. The more I experience in life, the more I understand that our success and significance in business is ultimately in direct proportion to the size of the contribution we make.

I'll never forget how Tony Robbins described my story and what we eventually used as his endorsement for *The Upside of Fear*. Although Mr. Robbins could have used a variety of ways to comment on my journey, he chose the following: "Congratulations on your turnaround from prison to *contribution*."

Notice he didn't say "business" or "financial success" or "a house in Maui." In his eyes, the significance of what I had done was the *contribution*. Over the years, I have made the commitment to reach out and inspire those who are struggling with the same problems I struggled with. I am also motivated by my responsibility to help others improve their sales careers and businesses.

So find your contribution. Consider whom you will help when you achieve your financial, personal, and professional dreams. Who else will benefit besides you? How will you respond when you are called upon?

Committing to use your prosperity to help others will provide with you a passion and calling beyond the scope of your sales career. It will help you see yourself in the larger perspective and find significance in your prosperity beyond your immediate family and community.

Because of my background and story, I receive many requests from jails, prisons, and other institutions to speak. I consider it my duty to accept these invitations whenever possible, and my staff knows that these requests receive priority, even though these institutions have no budget for a speaker.

Recently I went in to speak at a prison where I served time as a young man 25 years ago. Before I spoke to the "fellas," the warden had me escorted to the very cell house where I was housed in 1988. As I stood in the cell house, memories of the hopelessness I felt came over me in waves. We walked up the stairs and down the tier lined with cells and vacant stares.

When we approached the very cell in which I had lived, an officer signaled to the control center to open the door. When it opened, I stepped in and the door closed behind me. It was a visceral reaction. I struggled to control my nerves as I thought about how much my life had changed.

As I struggled with the emotions that overwhelmed me, I spoke to two groups of men, who, like me 25 years earlier, were searching for a way out. One of the men in the group remembered me from when he and I served time together many years ago. He approached me and said, "You always said you were going to do amazing things, and now you have." As we embraced, he began to weep and whispered, "If you can do it, so can I."

That day served as a potent reminder of how far I have come and how my journey can inspire others to change. Whether you realize it or not, eventually your journey will give others hope and confidence.

I was recently invited to speak to a group of female inmates who were involved with a wonderful program called "The 7 Habits on the Inside," an adaptation of Dr. Covey's landmark work for inmates in correctional institutions.

My schedule the week of the speech was insane: On Monday morning, I did two hours of *live* training on Prosperity TV. On Tuesday I flew to Austin, Texas, for a one-day sales training event with the legendary Tom Hopkins. That night I flew to Washington, DC, then on to Harrisburg, Pennsylvania. From the airport in Harrisburg, I drove to my hotel, arriving at midnight. The next morning, I spoke to a group of business owners and sales professionals. As soon as I finished there, I drove to Philadelphia, where I spoke for several hours that evening.

I flew back to Denver on Thursday morning and arrived at the airport at about 9:00 AM. I then drove 1.5 hours to my office and spent an hour with my staff. After that, I drove up to my home in the mountains—about 20 miles west of the city. I rested for about an hour at home, then got ready to travel to the women's prison about 1.5 hours south.

When I pulled into the prison parking lot at 5:00 PM, I was so tired I could barely see straight. As I entered the facility and waited in the prison visiting room for the guards to bring the women in, I seriously wondered if I had overextended myself. However, any hint of doubt disappeared the moment I began speaking. I knew immediately that I was in the exact place I was supposed to be. The look of hope and excitement on the women's faces was inspiring. They were committed to changing the course of their lives and were passionate about implementing *The 7 Habits* principles.

The point is that we all have an obligation to serve others, and sometimes we must put the needs of others before our own desires. On that evening, I wanted more than anything to just go home and crash. But I did what I had promised to do and helped countless individuals—including myself—by doing so.

As you grow and prosper in your life and business, the opportunities to expand your "circle of influence" will certainly grow. I remember thinking when I first read about the circle of influence in *The 7 Habits* that I had maybe a one in a million chance to go from the isolation of my prison cell to influencing others to do or be something good. Yet nowadays, I hear regularly from individuals and organizations about how their lives and businesses have prospered as a result of my service and work.

You are much closer to having a significant impact on others' lives than you may think. Take time to focus on the contribution you will make in the world once you achieve your aspirations. Ask yourself, how will I leave my mark? What will be my legacy?

Put it in the box, and one day you'll look up to see you've pulled it out and made a profound difference in other people's lives.

At this point in the focus step, you should have a pretty good idea of what you want, what you want to become, and what you want to contribute in your life and business.

If you have not taken the time to be really specific about all of these things, I strongly recommend you take the time to do that now. Even if you're one of those folks who tends to read books and skip over the exercises, consider whether or not you will create the results you want if you are unwilling to take consistent action with respect to the fundamentals of creating your prosperity plan.

It simply isn't enough to give these things cursory consideration and then move on. Take some time to get clear about them. Jot down some notes and ideas, even if it's just a word or two to describe what you want, what you want to become, and what you want to contribute.

You'll need this information to craft your prosperity plan, which you will implement on a consistent basis to create the life and business of your dreams.

What You Need to Do to Accomplish These Things in Life and Business

Once you have identified what you want in life and business, it's time to identify what you need *to do* to get there. This is a critical step in the process of creating an exceptional life and business—and it is also the step at which many of us fall short. Figuring out what we want is a fairly straightforward process. Getting it done is much more difficult, and it's where the rubber meets the road.

We will discuss how to consistently do these things in the next step; our purpose here is to identify which things we should do. It's about pinpointing priorities and deciding which actions will create the biggest impact.

There is an axiom that "Winners do what losers are not willing to do." It's not that losers don't *want* the same things winners want; it's that losers are *not willing* to take action and follow through in the same way that winners are.

If you have struggled with taking consistent action to get what you want in life, both personally and professionally—in other words, if you have struggled with the *doing*—it's probably due to one or both of the following reasons.

Reason 1 for these shortcomings is that "the confused mind says no." This refers to our tendency to do nothing when we become overwhelmed with too much to do.

Most of us have lists right now in our home or office with a gazillion things that we need to do or that need to happen before we move forward with an idea or project. Unfortunately, it's easy to become overwhelmed with this seemingly endless list of to dos, which usually causes us to become paralyzed and do nothing.

You've probably heard of the Pareto principle or the so-called 80/20 rule. This says that 80 percent of your results come from 20 percent of your efforts. It's a very useful tool to simplify our to-do lists and make progress toward our goals and aspirations. The key is to focus your efforts on the activities that produce the most significant results. I refer to these as *leveraged actions*—simple acts that produce extraordinary results that are the key to generating powerful outcomes in life and business. We will discuss which actions to take a little later in this chapter.

People also tend to wait until everything is perfect before they take action. But waiting for everything to be just right before taking the plunge on a project will likely leave you waiting for a long, long time. Circumstances are rarely ever perfect. Creating an exceptional life and business requires taking action in the face of adversity, not in its absence.

That being said, it is critical during this process to *simplify* things so that we're focusing on just one or two actions that will move us closer to our desired outcome. There will be plenty of time to take care of other details; the key at the beginning is to get going and create momentum as quickly as possible.

When I decided to open my first business in 2004—a residential heating and air-conditioning company—I honed in on hundreds of things that I needed to do before we could cut the ceremonious grand opening ribbon. The business needed a location, trucks, inventory, and office equipment. I had to recruit, hire, and train office staffers, service technicians, and installation experts. I needed to set up an accounting department, obtain the appropriate licensing, and get liability, workers' compensation, and unemployment insurance. I needed a marketing plan, a sales system, and countless operations' processes. There were literally hundreds, if not thousands, of things to do—so many, in fact, that it was easy to get lost in the confusion of what to do next. It was a small company that didn't have the luxury of a large staff to perform the myriad of tasks.

So instead of getting buried in minutiae, I decided to discern which leveraged activities that would generate the most immediate and powerful results. Relying on the basic business philosophy of IBM founder Thomas Watson Sr. that "Nothing happens until something gets sold," I decided to focus my attention on selling something. But before I could sell anything, I needed a sales lead.

Without an office, an employee, or a service truck, I took out a full-page ad for our new company in our Sunday newspaper announcing "our lowest prices ever!" (Since I hadn't been in business the day before, that was a completely honest claim.) At the bottom of the ad, I put the words "Call NOW! Operators standing by 24 hours a day—7 days a week."

I was the operator, the phone number was a cell phone, and I was definitely "standing by" in the living room, waiting for calls.

I set 16 sales leads on that Sunday and never looked back. Within 60 months the company had sold, serviced, and installed more than $20 million of residential heating and air-conditioning services and products. If I had waited until everything was set up and ready to go, I'd still be waiting.

To be successful, you have to take action—sooner rather than later. It doesn't have to be the perfect action; it just needs to be *action*. And the key to success is being able to decide which actions to take, since you usually a have quite a few to choose from. In fact, you frequently have too many choices. This, as we know, can be a real problem, since as we learned, the confused mind says "*no!*" That's when nothing happens, nothing changes, and dreams remain confined to the imagination. Without action, we don't create anything—ever.

With that discussion as a backdrop, let's figure out what specific steps you need to take to create what you want, what you want to become, and what you want to contribute in life and business.

Take each item you jotted down during the focus step so far and write down just one or two things that, if done on a consistent basis, would likely result in your desired outcome. Don't worry about identifying *everything* that you could or should do, just note one or two actions that will generate immediate and powerful results.

Remember: *Keep it simple!* The lion's share of your results will come from just a handful of your actions.

Let's work with an example or two.

Suppose you jotted down that your sales and business career goal is to earn an annual income of $200,000.

Stop and consider where you are in relation to that dream at this point in your life. What are the first steps you need to take to make that dream a reality? Are you at a point in your life where you already have a career and only need to grow your business to get there? Or are you at a stage where the first thing you need to do is learn the process of selling?

Because everyone is at a different stage professionally, what you need to do to reach your dreams depends on where you are right now. A successful salesperson may need only to increase his number of cold calls to reach a $200,000 income, whereas someone else may need to start by learning the basics.

Since my journey to creating wealth and prosperity began in a prison cell, I had a very long way to go. However, the key was not the length of my journey, but, instead, where I started. Your journey will begin at a different point than everyone else's; the key is identifying the first one or two steps you need to take to get started. As the ancient Chinese philosopher Lao-tzu once said, "A journey of a thousand miles begins with a single step." Where you begin the journey to reach your dreams is far more relevant than how far you need to go.

Your first step to achieving an exceptional sales and business career is far more important than your next step—because there is no next step until you take that first one. Therefore, this is where you need to focus you energy and action.

Beneath each item you listed, write the most important one or two things you should do.

If the goal is a $200,000 income, jot down what you need to do based on where you are in relation to that dream. It might look something like this:

What I want: a $200,000 annual income
What I need to do: study sales books and master the art of
    sales

or:

What I want: a $200,000 annual income
What I need to do: get more referrals, improve closing skills,
    and consistently serve my clients with passion and purpose

What you need to do depends on where you are in relation to the dream. Again, don't worry at this point about how far you may have to go to reach your dreams. Think only about where you have to start. That's all that matters right now.

It's important to break these to-do steps down into specific and simple actions as you identify each one.

For example, what specific things do you need to do to earn $200,000 in sales income? Break it down into the number of calls you need to hit your target. Let's say your average commission on each sale is $500, and your average closing ratio is 25 percent. That means you need 400 sales at $500 each to earn $200,000. If your closing ratio is 25 percent, you'll need to make 1,600 sales calls to net 400 sales. If you break down the 1,600 calls over approximately 250 working days a year, you'll need to make about 6 calls per day.

Because you've specified exactly what you need to do, you can easily see that you need to make six calls per day. With this new, specific information, your list might look like this:

What I want: a $200,000 annual income
What I need to do: make six calls per day, every day, and
    improve closing skills

The more specific you are, the less overwhelmed you will feel. As we move through this process, you will see how being specific in the action step will make it easier to implement your plan. If the person in the preceding scenario consistently made the six calls required per day, what are the odds she would eventually reach her income goals? Pretty good! You simply can't do the right sales activities and accidentally create the wrong sales results. Again, the solution lies in the *consistency* with which she makes the six calls per day. We'll be talking a lot about how to take consistent action in later chapters, but for right now just remember: Keep it simple. Keep it focused.

As I mentioned earlier, the process of creating your personal prosperity plan can—and should—involve a lot more than income and sales and business goals. In fact, success in other areas of your life will enhance the enjoyment you get from your sales and business success. Let's take a brief look at how you can incorporate other important issues and use this process in a variety of areas of your life and business.

Suppose you want to lose 30 pounds. You'll likely need to do a lot to complete this goal, won't you? You will need to research how to create a healthy diet, purchase and prepare the foods, and discipline yourself to eat only those foods. You should also visit your doctor and find an exercise program to help you increase aerobic capacity, build muscle, and burn calories.

Or you could just start with walking a mile a day and stop eating dessert every day. Might that be a less complicated place to start?

Of course, it would—and like the example before, what you need to do depends on where you are in relation to health and nutrition goals. It's different for each person. The key is identifying what one or two things would produce immediate and powerful results.

It might look like this:

What I want: to lose 30 pounds
What I need to do: walk 1 mile three days a week and stop
    eating sweets

What can help you even more is doing the math to see the kind of effect this will have.

Walking 1 mile a day will burn about 100 calories (depending on someone's weight and the terrain), and skipping one dessert a day would eliminate another 300 calories (sometimes more!). Eliminating and/or burning 400 calories per day would equal losing 1 pound of fat every 9 days, since 3,500 calories is equal to 1 pound of fat. At that rate, you would lose the 30 pounds in 9 months. And there you have it!

Now ask yourself this question: What are the odds you would lose the 30 pounds if you consistently consumed 400 fewer calories per day than you burned? Pretty much 100 percent, because there's science behind it and because you're doing the right things to create these results. The only possible way you couldn't lose the weight would be not consistently consuming fewer calories (unless of course there is some other underlying medical condition or illness).

Once you complete your prosperity plan, you will learn how to implement these powerful little steps that can change everything in your life and business.

You're probably getting the picture now—keep it straightforward. The key is focusing on one or two simple things you should do to make your dream a reality.

Simply take each thing that you want in life and business and beneath each one write down one or two things (not *everything*) you need to do to get there. Again, we will organize this information into your prosperity plan in the next step, where you will also learn how to take consistent action on your plan. Right now, just stay focused on gathering the list of things you want in life and business.

Follow the same process as you work through what you want to become and what you want to contribute in life and business. List each item and then write down one or two things you should do to make it a reality.

One of the most important items on my list was becoming a more active, dependable father to my son, a better father than I had ever been before. There didn't seem to be much I could do, given my confinement, but I knew the key was doing *something*. I knew I had to take some sort of action that was consistent with being the father I wanted to be.

So beneath what I wanted to become, I wrote the one thing I could do:

What I want to become: an awesome father to my son
What I need to do: maintain a connection to him through
  weekly letters

The letters weren't much, but again, it was all I could do. And they had a powerful impact on my relationship with my son over the long term.

It's not about how big or grand the action is; it's about doing it consistently. I wasn't always able to visit or even talk on the phone with my son, but I did what I could do *consistently*. Once you figure out what you want to become, list one or two things that will assist you in getting there.

Keep in mind that our lives and careers are not defined by the big moments of recognition everyone sees. They are defined by the little moments of action or inaction *nobody* sees. In other words, winning a sales award one time that everyone sees will not have as much impact as consistently doing the little things (like consistently making six calls per day) that only you see.

Complete the same exercise with respect to what you want to contribute. You will find that you will be able to contribute even more as you move closer to the things you want and want to become.

Acquiring wealth and prosperity for the sake of wealth and prosperity will not deliver much satisfaction over time. However, if you can use this wealth and prosperity to make a contribution to others, you'll have the foundation for sustaining your enthusiasm and momentum.

What I want to contribute: help others who are struggling to create productive lives

What I need to do: create a stable, prosperous life for myself and create the resources necessary to help others

Completing this exercise will provide you with a detailed list of the things that will make life wonderful for you. You will have a clear picture of what your dreams will look like. Beneath each item, you will have one or two things written down that will move you closer to your dream.

Combining the items from our examples, the list might look something like this:

What I want: a $200,000 annual income
What I need to do: make six calls per day—every day—and improve closing skills

What I want: to lose 30 pounds
What I need to do: walk 1 mile a day and stop eating dessert

What I want to become: an awesome father to my son
What I need to do: maintain a connection to him through weekly letters

What I want to contribute: help others who are struggling create productive lives
What I need to do: create a stable, prosperous life for myself and create the necessary resources to help others

This is, of course, just a sample of a partial list. You can have as many items as you want on this list. Be creative. Use your imagination. Remember, you have it for a reason and a purpose: to give you a place to start your journey to wealth, happiness, and peace of mind. And this journey begins with a single step.

Now that you have a clear vision of your exceptional life and business—as well as a list of things you need to do to get there—the next step is to organize that information into your prosperity plan.

However, before we move on to that step, you must do one more thing: understand any limiting beliefs you have that may undermine potential success.

Limiting beliefs are the biggest obstacle between you and an exceptional life and business. There is no bigger threat to unimaginable wealth, happiness, and prosperity than the accumulation of restrictive beliefs that live in your box. Therefore, if you are going to reach your true potential in life and business, you must figure out what these are and start working on getting them out.

The biggest challenge to discovering and addressing your limiting beliefs is the fact that, by their very nature, they are difficult to recognize. The reason they're so limiting is because they're so subtle and hard to detect. They are camouflaged into the very fabric of your thought processes and way of life. After all, if you could discern them easily, it wouldn't be as hard to identify and discard them. But limiting beliefs work covertly and over time to convince you that they aren't the problem—you are. They will brilliantly disguise themselves as accurate think-ing, and they are so well disguised because they have been hiding in plain sight for many years, often since the beginning. Even before you intentionally developed your basic beliefs about life and business, these restrictive thoughts took root in your mind's fabric—and they began to fester.

These assumptions found their way into your box at a very early age. Any time something good happened to you, they were there to keep you in check and to keep the party from getting out of control. If you ever began to feel a little *too* con-fident that you could accomplish anything you wanted, they were there to bring you back to reality.

They are seeds of doubt and uncertainty, voices telling you to be realistic. They whisper warnings that the economy and cheap competitors will make your sales success impossible. They are the expectations for your life and business that someone else imposed on you.

Limiting beliefs can come from anywhere—your family, community, and others—and develop at any time. People didn't put them there to be malicious; rather, they were placed there to protect you, to make sure you aren't disappointed by expecting too much out of life. They are there to ensure you aren't hurt by unreasonable expectations the way others were hurt. They are there to keep you grounded.

These beliefs are the limitations that others who have accepted mediocrity unwittingly placed on you; they aren't yours. They belong to people who have surrendered, who have resigned themselves to their reality that exceptional goals are unreasonable.

And because they belong to others, you have the right to return them. You deserve to create your own expectations. You have the power to defy conventions.

But to do all of this, you must first find these beliefs and outwit them, despite their uncanny ability to prove to you that they aren't even there.

As you grew up, those around you deposited limiting beliefs into your box. You accepted them as truth and your reticular activating system (RAS) began the process of collecting information that reinforced what you learned. Eventually, that belief system became your only truth.

Sometimes you put limiting beliefs in the box yourself. Something happened, and your psyche misinterpreted the information. That misinterpretation then formed the basis of an inaccurate belief, which your RAS noticed and reinforced while filtering out the information that challenged the belief.

The RAS wants desperately to prove you right 100 percent of the time—for better or for worse. The ultimate impact on your life doesn't matter—only reinforcing what you thought and being right matters.

Once limiting beliefs become your truth, your RAS spends the rest of your life meeting that expectation. You will only find more of what you expect to find, and your results will never exceed your expectations.

That's why it's absolutely critical to examine your box for malignant limiting beliefs and address them. It's often impossible to completely remove them, so the best option is to inundate and overwhelm them with a powerful *new* belief system that will eventually take root as the old thoughts grow weak and die off.

The bottom line is this: You don't have to think everything you believe, and you don't have to believe everything you think. You can control what goes into and through your mind. You can become the captain of your thoughts.

Let's take a look at some common limiting beliefs that live in our thoughts as well as some specific examples that demonstrate their cunning, subtle nature.

Several years ago, I noticed some tendencies I had when it came to my diet: I usually filled my plate with large portions and would eat every speck of food in front of me. The belief that triggered these actions was buried deep down and influenced my behavior very subtly. In fact, I didn't even realize the behavior was dysfunctional. That's the nature of limiting beliefs: They are such a part of us that we often can't even see how out of whack they are.

Eventually I came to see that this attitude toward eating was causing problems in my life. The older I got, the more difficult it became for me to keep my weight down.

As I looked within and sought to discover the source of this tendency, I remembered how safe and secure I felt when my mother cooked for our family when I was a kid. There was something about the warmth and security of knowing my mother was cooking in the kitchen. As I thought back over this, I realized I was experiencing similar emotions as an adult when I had a lot of food on my plate.

Deep down, I had made an emotional connection between large amounts of food on my plate and feeling a sense of comfort, something that was still driving my behavior 30 years later.

As I thought about my portion sizes, I asked myself why I tended to eat everything on my plate, even after I was no longer hungry. I recalled that I was allowed to get up from the dinner table when I was a kid only after I "cleaned my plate." In fact, if I didn't clean my plate, not only was I not leaving the table, but I was informed that innocent children in Africa were going to starve to death and it would be my fault!

That's a pretty heavy burden for a seven-year-old. Here I was, 30 years later, scarfing down every bite of food because of thoughts and beliefs that had been placed my box when I was a kid. That's how powerful our thoughts and beliefs are. They find their way into our boxes and drive our behavior many years later.

Another limiting belief that had worked its way into my box and had a destructive impact on my life was my father's unfavorable opinions of wealthy individuals. I remember my dad calling all rich people "crooks" when I was a kid (something I mentioned in an earlier chapter). My father had a deeply held belief (that his *own* father had no doubt put into his box) that successful people became wealthy by cutting corners and taking advantage of others.

I honestly don't think it ever occurred to my father that honest, hardworking people create businesses to earn a fair profit and serve others' needs. If someone had money, they had screwed someone else. It was as simple as that.

As a result, I remember being very suspicious of people with successful companies as a kid. And the more successful they were, the more suspicious I was of them. I remember a family seafood restaurant we frequented when I was a teenager. The food was great and I always enjoyed eating there or getting a po'boy to go. The family seemed to have a great product and obviously did very well with their restaurant.

But my dad always used to say, "You know, son. Those guys are mafia."

That was my dad—always skeptical of others' successes.

As this stuff went in my box, I developed the same belief that "rich people were crooks." It comes as no surprise to me looking back over my life that I didn't grasp the significant moral and legal problems with breaking laws to acquire money. After all, "rich people are crooks." If I had to become a crook to get money too, then so be it.

Obviously, my father was not responsible for my choice to live a criminal lifestyle; that accountability belongs entirely to me. I do believe, however, that we all need to be careful about what we put into others' boxes, especially children's boxes.

Sometimes we put things in the box ourselves as adults, which are just as powerful as the things other people put in there when we are kids. One time at a live event, I was working with audience members to help them identify limiting beliefs that were undermining what each of them was trying to accomplish in their lives and businesses.

In the very front row was an attractive woman in her 40s who looked like she had it all together. I couldn't help but wonder what she was there to figure out. She finally began to participate with the group during the afternoon sessions. Her story illustrates how limiting beliefs, even completely irrational ones, can come to control our lives. As I recall, the conversation went something like this:

"Wally, I am trying to figure out why I struggle to finish things. I start something, make a little progress, and then give up. I just can't seem to finish things."

"Well that's interesting," I said. "You give the appearance of having your act totally together." (Sometimes we all do a great job of making others think we've got it all together when that is anything but the case!)

"Well," she continued, "I may not look like it on the outside, but I struggle with my confidence because I can't seem to finish things."

I began to ask her about her experiences as a young girl as it related to finishing things. That's a natural place to start, because as I mentioned earlier, so much of what we think and believe stems from what was put in our boxes when we were kids. However, we couldn't identify anything she learned as a kid that would seem to create this limiting adult behavior.

Then she began to talk about her relationship with her mother after she was grown. She shared with everyone how she and her mother argued as she went through her teenage years. As with many parents and teenagers, tempers flared and their relationship eventually soured.

In fact, this woman had moved out of her mother's house by the time she was in her late teens, and their relationship continued to deteriorate over the next several years. She and her mother went from arguing to not speaking at all. You could see the pain and regret in this woman's face as she thought back over her relationship with her mother.

Several years after she moved out, she realized how important her relationship with her mother was. So after years of estrangement, she reached out to her mother and rekindled their relationship. Living in different states, they initially spoke only on the phone. But after a short time, this woman decided to drive across the country to reunite with her mother face to face. Tragically, however, her mother passed away just before they could see each other.

This woman shared her heartbreaking story as she stood in the front row of a room full of strangers. The room fell silent when she finished. Everyone could feel her loss and regret.

Immediately I saw the limiting belief that had found its way into her thoughts as a result of her experience, and I asked her, "Do you see any connection between your inability to finish things today and what you may perceive as your failure to 'finish things' with your mother?"

Obviously, this woman was not responsible for her mother's passing. However, we have to remember that our emotions and actions are based on what we *think* is true, not necessarily what actually *is* true.

At first she didn't see the connection. But as we discussed it further, she eventually came to accept the possibility that she had developed an irrational belief that she could not allow herself to finish things today because she could not finish the most important thing in her life: her reunion with her mother.

She was held back by a sense of guilt. How dare she finish something today when she couldn't finish things with her mother.

These are all powerful examples of how limiting beliefs don't have to—and often do *not*—make sense. Rich people aren't really crooks. Kids in Africa won't really die as a direct result of what I eat or don't eat. This woman wasn't really responsible for what happened to her mother. But these assumptions hinder our ability to create exceptional lives and businesses, not because they are true, but because we believe they are.

Sometimes these limiting beliefs are based on our underlying opinions of sales professionals and the sales process. If you are in sales until a "real" job comes along, you will likely struggle and be only mediocre in your sales career. But if you embrace your sales career as an opportunity to serve others with pride and professionalism, you will likely see better income and sales results.

Identifying limiting beliefs that you picked up as an adult or a child is critical to getting your mind right and creating wealth, happiness, and peace of mind. Once you figure out what these beliefs are, you can then create empowering beliefs to counteract them. This is what we will do in the next step.

But first we must idenfity the limiting beliefs. Think about the areas in your life where you seek improvement, as well as what you've learned about those things over your lifetime. How are your limiting beliefs undermining what you are trying to accomplish as an adult in your life and business?

Again, these beliefs are difficult to find by their very nature. They are so woven into the fabric of your basic philosophy that you don't see them. It takes work—and a harsh dose of honesty—to find them, as well as a willingness to examine everything you think you know.

Look at the areas where you want to improve yet continue to struggle over and over again. It's a good bet that you have some junk in your trunk and have developed a limiting belief around that thing you want.

It can also be useful to ask others for their opinion about what you believe. Request that they give a completely honest opinion about a certain belief you hold dear—and be prepared to hear things that may challenge you. Your RAS will go on high alert. Be careful as well to closely examine beliefs held by others who come from the same background as you, since they're likely to have the same junk in their trunk that you do.

Whether you look internally or seek feedback from others in your life, you must examine the thoughts and beliefs that you keep proving correct. They might be wrong or holding you back. They might be undermining everything you are trying to accomplish as an adult.

You don't have to allow yourself to be hindered by others' beliefs. And this isn't about blaming anyone. It's certainly not about getting therapy with your parents or settling old scores. It's about identifying things that you believe, that may be holding you back, and revamping the way you see these things.

You don't have any limits except the limits you think you have—and you have to dig deep to discover these. And when you do, you have to take some time to consider these issues. Don't gloss over them. What did you learn about money when you were a kid? What have you learned as an adult about business? What did you learn about sales? Most important, what have you learned about what is possible for you?

Did someone or some situation place limits on you? It's up to you to identify and get rid of these limitations. You can change all of it. It doesn't have to limit your life today.

You should now have a pretty thorough list of what you want, what you want to become, what you want to contribute, what you need to do, and what limiting beliefs may be undermining your success in life and business. The next step is to start organizing this information into your prosperity plan. You will assemble this and then review it during your daily quiet-time ritual.

You will revisit what you want, what you want to become, and what you want to contribute. You will determine what one or two things you must do on a consistent basis to create an exceptional life and sales career. And you will create new beliefs and thoughts to challenge the limiting beliefs you've developed in your past. You will know what a perfect life and business look like for you—and you will know how to get there.

The next step in the FEAR process is to create and get deeply emotionally committed to your prosperity plan.

CHAPTER FIVE

Step 2: Emotional Commitment

There is one quality which one must posses to win, and that is definiteness of purpose, the knowledge of what one wants, and a burning desire to possess it.

—Napoleon Hill

Step 2 of the upside of FEAR process is getting powerfully *emotionally committed* to your income and sales goals, as well as any other goals you identified in the focus step. This commitment step also begins the process of moving from *planning* your exceptional life and business to actually *taking actions* toward making it your new reality. This is where you will move from knowing and wanting to *doing*.

Think back to a memory from your childhood that sticks with you even today. Once you've recalled a specific memory, consider how long it took you to recall it. A millisecond? For most people, it doesn't take long. We can recall something that happened decades ago instantly if it's important enough to us.

Now ask yourself this question as you think about that specific memory: What were you doing an hour before or an hour after the moment in the memory? If you're like most folks, you can't remember.

Isn't that something? Despite having such a clear, precise memory of something that happened when you were a kid, you can't remember what you were doing just before or just after.

More than 400 million seconds elapse from the moment you are born through your thirteenth birthday. And if you assume that each second that ticks by is a potential memory, then that's 400 million potential moments to remember. Yet you remember only a handful of things from your childhood.

There's a reason we remember a small number of things from our childhood over the course of so many years. It's because of emotion. Memories are created when something that creates a strong emotion occurs; then, that event anchors to that emotion.

Once that happens, decades can go by and you can still recall that moment at the drop of a hat.

Therefore, there's a very good chance that you were feeling a powerful emotion during the memory you just recalled. You were likely very happy, very sad, very scared, or very *something*. It's the emotional state you were experiencing in that moment that binds your memory to the event and ensures that you'll never forget it.

Sometimes the memory is one we would rather forget, but we can't. Once that memory is programmed into your subconscious mind, it's not going anywhere—ever.

That's the permanent effect of forming a powerful emotional connection to something: It's there for the rest of your life. And even though you weren't consciously thinking about it before you started reading this chapter, it was right there on the surface of your subconscious mind just waiting to be called up at a moment's notice.

The goal of the emotional commitment step is to program everything you listed in the focus step into your subconscious mind, just like a powerful childhood memory. This will ensure that these items are deeply embedded in your subconscious mind. The items on your prosperity plan will be ever present in your subconscious mind.

In addition, it will drive your daily behavior to do the things you identified as needing to be done to get the things you want. No matter how distracted your conscious mind becomes, your subconscious mind and your reticular activating system (RAS) will be aware of where you are going and what you need to get there. You will move toward your ultimate destination automatically—in the same way you drive from your office to your home without consciously thinking about it.

Later, in the action step, you will learn about cognitive dissonance and how this tendency of human nature will drive your actions to consistently do the things you already know you should be doing. And when you think and do the right things, success is not a matter of *if;* it is a matter of *when.*

Have you ever started a new diet and stuck to it for a few days, only to forget you are on a diet at some point and blow it? I don't mean you consciously decided to break your diet; I mean you were actually several bites into a piece of cake when you thought to yourself, "Holy cow! I completely forgot that I was on a diet!"

Wouldn't it have been great to have the diet programmed into your subconscious mind as a powerful memory? That way, no matter how distracted you became, the knowledge that you are indeed dieting would be right there on the surface of your subconscious, just like that childhood memory from 30 or 40 years ago. You'd be a lot less likely to forget you are on a diet and shove that yummy stuff down your piehole.

Similarly, have you ever decided to do something new in your sales career that you absolutely knew would have a profound impact on your income? You were out of your mind with excitement, made the decision to do it, and went to work and did it. Boom! That's it. This is your new way of doing things—and it's going to change your business forever!

Soon enough, however, you were distracted by the usual daily tasks and problems that needed to be solved. It takes only about a week before you forget about the new way of doing things and go back to whatever you were doing before. The worst part is that the new results of increased profitability and/or income would have manifested if you had implemented the change over the long term. But somewhere along the way, you forgot you were doing the new thing and things went right back to where they were.

Wouldn't it have been nice if you had programmed this new approach into your subconscious mind so that no matter how busy you got, you could never forget you were doing it? Even if you *wanted* to forget it, you couldn't.

Imagine the impact on your business and the results you'd see if you actually did that new thing consistently.

You know by now that you can't focus on creating one thing and accidentally create something else. (Remember the motorcycle parts in the box?) If you focus on the new way of doing things at work, you will create only the desired results of those things.

The problem is that most of us rely on willpower alone to keep us on track. But as we so frequently discover, our willpower will fail us—and we simply stop doing the things we know we need to be doing. The secret to creating an exceptional life and business is to program your subconscious mind with everything you identified in the previous focus step *as a permanent memory*. Once you do that, everything in life you want, want to become, and want to contribute will be permanently etched into your subconscious thought and memory. You won't be *able* forget to do the things you know you need to do, nor will your RAS filter out opportunities you need to make your dreams a reality. You also won't have to rely on willpower alone. You will supplement your willpower to make a certain number of cold calls or follow that process at work with a powerful memory. It will become part and parcel of who you are, and you will not forget.

And as you'll see in the action step later, once these things are etched into your memory, they will guide your actions to remain congruent (consistent) with the things on which you are now focused. Once those actions become consistent actions, they will weave the fabric of who you are and turn into habits. The results will soon follow.

The key is to supplement your conscious thought and willpower with a powerful emotional connection to the things you are focused on and expect in your life and business. This requires that you program your goals as an unforgettable *permanent memory into your box*.

The following is a three-step process that will get you emotionally committed to your dreams and make them permanent memories. This process will help you organize the information from the previous step into your prosperity plan. The three steps are:

1. Write it.
2. Review it.
3. Feel it.

Let's go into each of these in detail.

Write It

The first step is to write out those three crucial goals: what you want, what you want to become, and what you want to contribute. You'll also outline the things you listed that you must do to get the things you want. You should have this list from the previous step, and this will form the basis of your prosperity plan.

The key here is to write those things out as statements of fact in present tense. In essence, you are going to manufacture the thoughts as if you have already achieved the goals and aspirations you are writing down. This will drive the emotions and actions to make them actually happen. It's all one huge circle of creativity and manifestation—basically, a self-fulfilling prophecy.

It's important to understand that even if the thoughts are manufactured, the emotions, actions, and results that flow from the thoughts are as real as real gets. Therefore, as you begin programming your thoughts about your sales and business career, you'll engage in a physiological process that creates the emotion. And although the thoughts are manufactured initially, the emotions that result are *real*.

In other words, if you think you won the lottery, you will experience the exact same emotions as if you actually won the lottery, even if you later learn you did *not* win the lottery. The emotions created in the moments you thought you won the lottery are real.

Remember the story of the two teenage girls in the car accident? Each family experienced the emotions connected to what they *thought* had happened, not what turned out to have actually occurred. This is why it's crucial for you to write out your prosperity plan in the present tense, as though it is actually true.

Let's take a couple of examples. Suppose you identified a $200,000 annual income as one of your career goals. You write out the following in present tense on your prosperity plan:

I earn $200,000 annually.

We will refer to each of the things you outline in your personal prosperity plan as *consistency outcomes* and to the things you will need to do to reach these outcomes as *consistency actions*.

It's important to describe the consistency outcomes in a way that feels right to you; don't limit yourself according to my words or anyone else's description. Use the words that feel natural to you, and *keep it simple!* Don't worry at this point about *how* you are going to accomplish these things. We'll get to that. What's critical now is that you write out specifically what you want in your life and business *as if it has already happened.*

Incidentally, you can use this process in each area of your life and business that is important to you: your income, your business, your professional aspirations, your health and physical fitness, your relationships, and so on.

Now move on to what you want to become and what you want to contribute in life and business. Be specific.

Here are two specific examples from my own experience:

I am an awesome father to my son.

and

I am a man of honor and character.

Your contributions might include:

I have built three schools in Ethiopia.

or

I have adopted two Chinese orphans.

or

I have donated $1,000,000 to charity.

The key is to write them in present tense, as if you have already achieved them. Do not worry about how far away the dream may seem, or that it might be too extravagant. It isn't.

When you are finished dreaming as big as you can dream... *go bigger!* Don't let people who tell you, "You can't do that," get in your way while you are busy doing it!

Each consistency outcome that you've written out will be a heading on your prosperity plan. Next, you will begin to fill in one or two things you need to do on a consistent basis to make each dream your reality. These are your consistency actions. While each item on your prosperity plan is a desired *outcome or result*, each consistency action is what you'll *need to do* to get there.

Write the consistency actions out in present tense, as if you are already doing them on a consistent basis, just as you did the consistency outcomes. For example, using the income goal from earlier, your consistency outcome and consistency actions might look like this:

I earn $200,000 per year. *(consistency outcome)*
1. I make six new cold calls per day. *(consistency action #1)*
2. I run every sales opportunity with passion and purpose. *(consistency action #2)*

Once you have written out your consistency outcomes and consistency actions, you will have the foundation for creating everything you want in life and business. All your personal and professional success will emanate from your plan.

How likely is it you will achieve your consistency outcome if you implement the consistency actions every day? I'd say the odds are pretty good! The key, of course, is taking regular, habitual actions, which we will discuss later. Right now, we are concerned only with creating your prosperity plan.

Let's take another example. Suppose one of the things you want is to build a $10 million business, and you have identified two leveraged actions that will help you get there. Write out the consistency outcomes and actions like this:

My company generates $10 million in annual revenue. *(consistency outcome)*
1. I generate 2,000 new sales leads per year. *(consistency action #1)*
2. I treat my customers and employees with dignity and respect. *(consistency action #2)*

Again, outline what success looks like to you, use words that feel personal and comfortable, and don't get overwhelmed with the how. Just stay focused on what you want and what steps will likely get you there.

Here is another example from other areas you may be focused on:

I weigh 180 pounds. *(consistency outcome)*
1. I eat only healthy foods. *(consistency action #1)*
2. I exercise three days per week. *(consistency action #2)*

Is there any doubt that if you ate only healthy foods and exercised on a consistent basis that you would enjoy a healthier, more active lifestyle? Of course not! You already know that; you just aren't doing it. But that will all change once you leverage *The Power of Consistency.*

Once you have written down each consistency outcome and one or two consistency actions under it, you will have created a very simple, straightforward personal prosperity plan. This will be the foundation on which you will create amazing things in your life.

Keep in mind at this point that you need to identify only one or two actions that will lead to your desired outcomes. Although there are likely dozens of potential actions, just figuring out what one or two you'll act upon will move you toward your desired outcomes.

This is also your opportunity to outline consistency outcomes that are specifically designed to counteract the limiting beliefs you discovered in the focus step of this process. You will learn later how to program these things into your subconscious mind. When you do that, you will inundate any limiting beliefs in your box with powerful new beliefs that will help you overcome them and inspire you to achieve amazing things in your life and business.

Suppose, for example, that you've always believed that the profession of sales is a shady one and that you can't trust sales professionals. To counteract that limiting belief, you could add a consistency outcome and consistency action, like this:

The sales profession is an honorable career. *(consistency outcome)*
    1. I extend myself professionally to better serve my clients. *(consistency action)*

Let's consider another example of how you can overpower a previously held limiting belief with new beliefs.

Suppose you've always assumed that "rich people are crooks." Let's further suppose that this limiting belief was undermining your ability to create legitimate wealth and success. If that were the case, you could add consistency outcomes and actions like the following:

> Creating wealth while serving others and creating value is an honorable endeavor. *(consistency outcome)*
> 1. I consistently extend myself professionally to others in service. *(consistency action)*
> 2. I consistently seek to provide exceptional value. *(consistency action)*

Once this new set of thoughts and beliefs is programmed into the subconscious memory, it will bury any dysfunctional beliefs about creating wealth and prosperity. When you are finished with your freshly minted personal prosperity plan, you could have something that looks like this, depending on how many areas of your life you want to address:

My Prosperity Plan
I earn $200,000 per year.
1. I make six new cold calls per day.
2. I run every sales opportunity with passion and purpose.

I create wealth while serving others. Creating wealth is an honorable endeavor.
1. I consistently extend myself professionally to others in service.
2. I consistently seek to provide exceptional value.

I weigh 180 pounds.
1. I eat only healthy foods.
2. I exercise three days per week.

I am an awesome husband and father.
1. I make time for my family on a weekly basis.
2. I treat my wife with patience and kindness.

I am a man of honor and character.

1. When I give my word, I have given my bond.
2. I resolve conflict with fairness and equity.

I improve the life of others who are struggling.

1. I share what I have learned when called upon.

Your list can be as long or as short as you want, and you can add or delete from the list as you desire. In fact, you will learn in the action step about the two times you will delete consistency outcomes from your list: when you accomplish them or when you fail to take the appropriate consistency actions (more on that later).

The thing to keep in mind the entire time is that this is a *creative process*, so don't get hung up on format or rules or perfection. Write things out so that they have significance and meaning to you. Whatever way you do it is the "correct" way. The goal is for you to end up with a plan that you will learn to review during your quiet-time ritual and program into your subconscious mind.

And remember to dream *big*. Don't be restrained by practical expectations. Be *unreasonable!* Allow your imagination to explore the possibilities. Remember, you have the ability to see things that you haven't created yet and dream things you haven't accomplished yet. Use your ability to do that!

Seeing the life and business of your dreams is the first step toward creating them. Embrace Dr. Stephen R. Covey's words: "All things are created twice."

Also keep in mind that you don't need to *know* everything you need to do to accomplish your dreams. As you make progress and discover new things you need to do, you can add those. But don't get overwhelmed in minutiae or lost in the details. Keep the big picture in mind. Pick the low-hanging fruit. Make this process easy on yourself, and above all, *keep it simple!*

You have reached an important milestone at this point in the process and have done what only a very small percentage of people have done by outlining what a perfect life for you will look like and one or two things that you need to do on a consistent basis to get there. Most people don't even know where they will end up, much less how they plan on getting to wherever it is they are going. They are ships drifting at sea with no focus, direction, or plan. They are lost, and their futures are in doubt. They never think about the things they are thinking about.

But you, my friend—you are different. By taking the time to seriously consider what you want, what you want to become, and what you want to contribute in life and business—and by outlining precisely what you need to do to get there—you have distinguished yourself from the masses. You have taken a significant step toward becoming "the master of your destiny" and "captain of your soul." You have taken control over where you are going and how you are going to get there. Of course, you have more work to do, but you have taken the first critical step on your journey to wealth, happiness, and peace of mind.

You have taken an enormous step and displayed strength of character and determination to create the life and business you deserve. You have a right to live the life you have written out. All you have to do now is take consistent steps toward achieving the goals on your prosperity plan.

In the next phase of this process, you will learn how to program your prosperity plan into your subconscious memory. Once it's embedded there, you will never forget what you are working on and what you need to do to get there. You'll learn about a quiet-time ritual that will result in programming your prosperity plan into your subconscious memory and getting you deeply emotionally committed to your dreams. It will propel you to take consistent action toward reaching your dreams.

Review It and Feel It

Reviewing your prosperity plan—and experiencing the emotions of creating your exceptional life during a daily quiet-time ritual—is a critical part of reaching your income and career goals. In fact, if you don't commit to a 15-minute quiet-time ritual, the excitement you feel while writing out your plan will be a fleeting moment of potential that never moves beyond your imagination.

Although you create your dreams in your imagination first, you certainly don't want to leave them there. You want to see that creation eventually reveal itself in your life and business. And your daily 15-minute quiet-time ritual will provide that bridge between dreams and reality.

Not only will you find strength and inspiration in these moments, but you will also form an abiding emotional connection with your dreams during this time. Your dreams will take on new significance, and you will come to know that they are destined to come true. The time you spend alone in thought will guide and direct your daily actions to ensure that what you *do* is consistent with what you *want*. When your thoughts, emotions, and actions are in alignment, the results are certain.

More important, by programming your consistency actions in to your subconscious (your box), cognitive dissonance will drive you to take those steps daily.

I realize, of course, with all the distractions of work, family, bills, and chores, it will be difficult to find 15 minutes a day to devote to your dreams. But you have to do it—even though it is difficult. Think of all the times when you have given yourself to others. Surely you can find just 15 minutes a day for yourself.

You may need to dig down deep to get this done. It's the fundamental process that requires you to completely reprogram the contents of your box. Fifteen minutes a day devoted to you and your dreams can change the course of your life. Fifteen minutes a day can supplement your willpower and give you the strength to do the things you need to do to have the things you want to have. Fifteen minutes a day is the one thing that will change *everything*.

We know that, according to Albert Einstein, "We can't solve our problems at the same level of thinking that created them." Your quiet-time ritual is what you use to elevate your thoughts to a higher level.

There is simply no escaping the necessity of getting alone with your thoughts if you want to see *The Power of Consistency* manifest itself in your life and business. You cannot reap the harvest if you don't plant and tend the seed—and that is what your quiet-time ritual is for.

Most important, it is about *you*, not about your spouse or your boss or your business partners. It's about 15 minutes a day that belongs to you and only you—15 minutes that will change your life and the course of your destiny.

William Jennings Bryan once said, "Destiny is no matter of chance. It is a matter of choice. It is not a thing to be waited for; it is a thing to be achieved." Your 15-minute quiet-time ritual is how you choose your new destiny.

Will you struggle initially to wake up 15 minutes early or to stay awake 15 minutes longer to do your quiet-time ritual? Maybe. But do it anyway, despite this initial struggle.

Find the time wherever you can: in the morning, before you go to sleep, during lunch or a break at work, while waiting for the laundry, or even while waiting for a meeting.

Just find the time. *If you don't find the time, you won't find the results you desire in your life and business.*

Your quiet-time ritual is the missing link to everything you've ever wanted and wanted to accomplish in your life and business. This is what you've been looking for—15 minutes a day to create unimaginable wealth and success in your life and business.

Seems like a small price to pay, doesn't it?

I'd like to share with you the morning routine I use to program my thoughts, emotions, actions, and results. This brief quiet-time ritual completely changed everything in my life; it served as the foundation for the massive transformation that lifted me from living in a cold prison cell behind concrete and razor wire to a life of wealth and prosperity.

I tend to awaken early in the mornings so that I can have a little "me time" before the hectic pace of life gets a foothold. I walk into the living room and build a fire (which, at my house, involves hitting a switch on the wall that somehow sends fire to the fire place—it's amazing). My home is high in the Rocky Mountains of Colorado at nearly 9,000 feet elevation, so it's chilly in the mornings year-round—and the fire makes for a warm, inviting place to have some quiet time.

And just in case you are thinking, "Well, yeah. It's easy for you. You have a cozy place to sit by a fire and gaze out at the beautiful mountains," keep in mind that for the first seven years, I awakened each morning in a cold, concrete bunker called a prison cell. I would sit quietly on my steel bunk surrounded by misery and austerity. I didn't have that fireplace then—and I certainly wasn't looking out at the mountains.

Yet despite my reality, I imagined the life that awaited me beyond prison walls. I imagined the life of wealth and prosperity that was my new destiny. I pictured the life I would one day have with my son.

Once the fire is built, I make my coffee and turn on the stereo to a very low volume and tune it to the "Spa" or "Zen" channel on satellite radio. I sit down in a chair next to the fireplace and turn on a soft lamp. As I sit quietly, soaking up the warmth of the fire and listening to the soft music, I revel in the moment. I don't regret the past or wonder about the future. I am completely absorbed in the moment.

It's very easy for us humans to relive past frustrations and hurts or to fret over the uncertain future. There will be plenty of time for that later. But right now, it's about *right now*.

Even before I really get started, this is my favorite time of the day. I wish it could last for hours. But, alas, at some point I will have to participate in the world around me.

I sit quietly and peacefully and take a few moments to count my blessings. There is something about gratitude that gets my day off to a good start and puts me in a wonderful state of mind. I think about the wonderful things I have received in my life: my family, my successful companies, my health, my smart and committed staff, freedom, and so on.

Again, lest you think it's easy for me to be grateful, I spent many years counting my blessings in a desolate cell. No matter how bad things were, I could always find something to be grateful for.

Also keep in mind I am not some kind of Zen Master. Ask anyone who knows me well, and they will tell you I am high strung and impatient. I do not want to suggest that I walk around in a robe with my eyes closed and hands open in supplication to the heavens in some ultra peaceful state.

My nature for 23 hours and 45 minutes a day couldn't be more different from my nature during my 15-minute quiet-time ritual. That's *why* it's so necessary for me. It grounds me and gives me strength and direction over the course of my day. It gives me sanity and peace of mind.

So although this type of quiet-time ritual is not natural for me, I have come to love it and look forward to it. I have also learned that it is a critical step to creating exceptional success in life and business.

After I've gotten comfortable and counted a few blessings, I take out my prosperity plan. At various times over the years, it's been on a notepad, on a computer, or even on the inside cover of a favorite book. It doesn't matter where it is—as long as it *is*.

I then review each consistency outcome and consistency action one at a time. After I read each outcome a few times, I close my eyes and imagine what it will look like once it's happened.

Remember: You have the ability to close your eyes and see something long before you've actually created it in your life and business. Use your ability to see it. Allow yourself to see the manifestation of the dream however it looks to you. There is no right or wrong; there is only how it looks to you. As the brilliant Dr. Wayne Dyer says, "You won't believe it when you see it. You'll see it when you believe it."

I remember years ago when I would review "I am an awesome father to my son" in my prison cell. I would close my eyes and repeat that consistency outcome and picture myself hugging my son and telling him that I love him and am proud of him.

I would then review the necessary daily consistency actions consistent with being an awesome father to him. My consistency actions at that time were "I write Hunter letters on a weekly basis" and "My word is my bond with my son." Given my incarcerated status, those were the only actions I could take that were consistent with being an awesome father. (We'll talk more about action in the next step.)

As you read each outcome, see what each one will bring to you: the house you'll live in; the business you'll grow; yourself as a healthy, physically fit individual; your relationships with others; the income you'll earn. Use your ability to *see* all of it. Remember: "All things are created twice."

As you read and see each outcome, repeat the consistency actions written below them. Allow the dream—and what you need to do to reach it—to seep into your subconscious mind. Additionally, allow yourself to experience the emotion as if these things have already happened. Something amazing often happens here: The emotions that you fabricate during your quiet-time ritual are just as real as the emotions you will feel when you actually achieve the dream.

As I reviewed my prosperity plan alone in my cell 15 years ago, I would imagine how it would feel when I became an awesome father to my son. Last August, I took my son to college. When it came time to leave him, I gave him a hug and told him how proud I was of him. He told me he was proud of me too. As we embraced outside his dormitory, I reveled in the moment—because it was just like I always dreamed it would be. That moment with my son felt exactly as it did when I imagined it alone in a cold prison cell 15 years earlier.

Thoughts—even imagined ones—are powerful forces for your emotions to feed off.

As you are reviewing your personal prosperity plan, you are literally *manufacturing* a new thought process—essentially putting new beliefs into your box. You will eventually remove these thoughts and beliefs as you take action.

Another critical process is taking place during this time as well. Remember how memories are made: Something happens and is anchored to an emotion. As you experience the emotions of reaching your dreams, you are attaching powerful emotions to the thoughts. And you are therefore creating a subconscious memory that will always be lurking beneath the surface—and that will have a profound impact on your actions with respect to your income and sales. It will have a profound impact on whether or not you forget you are on a diet and shove a piece of carrot cake in your mouth. It will have a profound impact on whether or not you remember that you should be making six sales calls per day to boost your career.

Those little consistent actions will have a powerful impact on your results in life and business. So allow yourself to experience the emotions of reaching your dreams as you picture each outcome in your mind's eye. Enjoy it. *Feel* it. As you do, you attach potent emotions to reaching your dreams and create powerful memories deep within your subconscious mind that will guide your actions in the next step. You won't forget the dreams and what you need to do to reach them when faced with distracting daily responsibilities.

You are programming the route from where you are today to where you want to end up into your subconscious, making them "second nature." And just like the trip from your office to your home, you will reach your destination—despite life's distractions. Regardless of anything that's happening in your conscious mind, your subconscious mind will stay focused on getting you where you deserve to be.

Common sense dictates that if you remain focused on achieving something, you will eventually get there. But daily distractions too often prevent your conscious mind from obsessing on success. This is why programming the destination into your *sub*conscious mind provides you with a guide that never gets distracted and never loses its way. You are setting the neurological anchors in your mind that will guide you naturally to begin taking your consistency steps.

Additionally, you will find yourself strengthened to take the consistent actions necessary to reach your dreams. Whatever those actions are, this guide will ensure that you're completing them, which will most certainly lead to the results you want in life and business. You'll see in the next chapter that failing to take one of the steps you have programmed will cause internal anxiety called cognitive dissonance, something that will drive you to new levels of consistency and performance.

You'll also see how creating your prosperity plan and programming it into your (subconscious) box is translated into amazing results through action.

CHAPTER SIX

Step 3: Action

Action is the real measure of success.

—Napoleon Hill

Will Rogers once said, "Even if you are on the right track, you'll get run over if you just sit there."

When it comes to creating wealth, happiness, and peace of mind in life and business, the rubber pretty much meets the road with action—because the only way to achieve your dreams in these arenas is to take consistent action toward them.

And that's the key: *consistent* action. It's not the scope, size, or drama of the action you take to achieve your dreams. Making a single grand gesture one time (usually) will not do you much good. Doing lots of little, helpful things regularly is what's going to make the difference.

As famed entrepreneur, author, and motivational speaker Jim Rohn famously said, "Success is doing ordinary things extraordinarily well." The single biggest cause of getting mediocre results is sales and business professionals' failure to do the small things repeatedly. We often become far too concerned with "elephant hunting"—searching for that one big kill— when success really requires brilliant execution of the small, seemingly insignificant activities in sales and business.

So don't get hung up on the amount or degree of actions you take as you evaluate what's necessary to reach your dream; *get hung up on the consistency of the action.* This is the quintessential example of how taking "baby steps" will get you where you want to go.

Earlier I referred to the ancient truth that "A journey of a thousand miles begins with a single step." It's not about the first step, or the tenth step. Wealth, happiness, and peace of mind are about the single next step.

The key is to ensure that you are moving in a consistent direction toward your dreams *today.* There is no need to worry about which steps you'll take tomorrow or next week. If you don't take the first step, there will be no next step. The challenge, of course, is mustering up the self-discipline to take each next step on a consistent basis. Jim Rohn also said, "Discipline is the bridge between goals and accomplishment." To get where you want to go from wherever you are, you must do the little things brilliantly—and consistently.

This is where things get a little tricky for us humans. If we could consistently *do* the things we know we *should* be doing, we would already be enjoying amazing lives of wealth and prosperity. (And chances are, you wouldn't be reading this book right now.)

But it isn't that simple. In fact, as you might remember from the Introduction, *that's* the essence of the conundrum of human nature: *knowing what you need to do to create wealth and prosperity in your life and business and failing to do it.*

If only we could just do the little things we know we should do. If we could just make six new cold calls every day, we could earn that six-figure salary—and life would be awesome!

After my father died in 1996, one of the items I put on my personal prosperity plan was to be an "awesome father to my son." But given my circumstances at the time—living behind bars—what actions could I take that would be consistent with being an awesome father to him?

I knew I couldn't do anything big. But fortunately for me, becoming an awesome father wasn't about doing something grand; *it was about doing something consistently*—even if that something seemed small and insignificant at the time.

So I decided to do the one thing I *could* do from my prison cell: write my son letters. And that's what I did. Over the next seven years, I wrote hundreds of letters to my son.

These letters didn't seem like much to a small boy who wasn't even old enough to read. He had another "daddy" in his life who was doing "big" things, like going camping or ice skating or visiting amusement parks. Compared with activities like that, writing letters seemed insignificant. But that turned out to be enough—as long as I kept at it.

Seven years after I entered prison, I walked out of it. By then, that little 3-year-old boy was 10, and as you might imagine, we didn't have the type of relationship we would have had if I had been a better man. But we had *something* as a result of those consistent letters.

My sole focus upon my release was to find my son and be the father he deserved. When I got out, I learned that Hunter's mother was in prison and that he was living with his aunt, who had always been a very positive and supporting influence in his life. Shortly after my release, I contacted her and eventually convinced her that I was a different man than the punk who had abandoned that little boy seven years earlier. Eventually she agreed that Hunter should be with me. My son grew up to become an amazing young man, and the relationship between the two of us grew stronger over the years.

Hunter understandably struggled with anger and abandonment issues for several years; however, he ultimately blossomed beyond the limitations I had created for him over his first 10 years. I know deep in my heart that the connection we maintained through those "little" letters was the basis on which we eventually formed a deep and loving relationship.

In my first book, I recounted a story where Hunter returned home from a visit with his mother's family. He had spent some time with his great grandmother, Nana, when he was 15 or 16 years old. He had been with me for many years by that time, and things were going well. Nana had seen to it that Hunter received the letters I had written him during the years I was incarcerated. However, when he returned home from that trip as a teenager, he had some letters Nana had discovered in her garage that he never received. These were letters I had written him 10 and 12 years earlier.

I described the day he came home with those letters:

Last summer as I worked in our yard, Hunter walked toward me with a stack of letters. "Look, Dad," he said. "Look at these letters you wrote when I was a kid." I stood with my son, now nearly a man, in the front yard of our mountain home on that glorious summer day, and read the letters with him. I thought back to twelve years earlier when I had written them in a dark lonely place, and I knew during that moment with Hunter that my life was fulfilled. The hard work and determination had paid off. It was all worth it.

Together we read the words I had written so many years before.

> *Hunter,*
> *You are truly an Angel Boy and you embody all that is hope, Joy, Love, Goodness, and Pure. There is no man on this planet more proud of his son than I am of you. I realize that I have made mistakes, and I am so sorry that I am separated from you, but one day I will be with you again, and NEVER again will I do anything that will result in my being apart from you.*
> *I LOVE YOU and that will NEVER change.*
>
> — *Love, Daddy*

With a smile, Hunter turned with the letters and walked away, knowing his father had always loved him.

While Hunter had received hundreds of the letters I had sent, somehow this stack of letters did not reach him until 12 years later. Ironically, it didn't even matter that he didn't get them years earlier. In fact, I believe the impact on him was even deeper because he received them as a young adult.

Time will expose or promote all of us. Eventually our actions—for better or for worse—will be revealed. Success depends on taking the right actions on a consistent basis, even if the results aren't created until years later. The bottom line is that you simply cannot do the *right* things and accidentally create the wrong results. Eventually, the results will reflect the actions.

I believe my relationship with my son—as well as the foundation on which he is building a successful life—is the result of *The Power of Consistency*.

All it took was a seemingly insignificant letter written to him on a consistent basis. Those small steps repeated over and over again generated powerful results. Today Hunter is in second year of college, and we have an amazing relationship, just like the one I used to imagine alone in my prison cell. He has reached the age where there is less parenting and more friendship. As he grew up and learned that he could count on his father, he gained the security and confidence to seek out his own journey. He is a remarkable young man with a very powerful story of his own. He saw and experienced things no child ever should, yet he transcended the struggle I created for him over the first 10 years of his life. Something tells me that one day he will have a significant impact on the lives of kids who are facing very difficult circumstances the way he did as a child.

You may have fallen short taking consistent action in the past, but here is a little news flash for you, my friend: You *can* still do the things you need to do, regularly and habitually, to create the life and business of your dreams. You just need a little help finding the strength to do the little things brilliantly and consistently.

Every single person knows what it's like to commit to doing something we know we need to do only to fall short after a short period of success. We just have a hard time sticking with it, right?

You get all excited about starting some new routine that you know will improve your life and business. And you know that "this is the time and now is the place." But somehow, within a few days, you go from making six cold calls to making one.

What happened? Where did all your determination go? How did your willpower and self-discipline fail you?

It's actually pretty simple to answer these questions—if you understand a little quirk about willpower.

Believe it or not, willpower is actually an exhaustible resource that loses strength over the short term. The more you use it, the weaker it becomes—and the less you can rely on it.

In their landmark bestseller, *Switch: How to Change Things When Change Is Hard*, authors Chip and Dan Heath describe a study that demonstrates how self-discipline weakens over time.

In a nutshell, the study outlines the impact using willpower now has on our future ability to draw on the same willpower. In the study, college students were asked to stay in a room with chocolate chip cookies and radishes. One group was allowed to eat the cookies but had to resist the radishes, and the other group was allowed to eat the radishes but had to resist the cookies.

Obviously, the group that had to resist the cookies had to exercise more willpower than the group who had to resist the radishes. Amazingly, the group that used this resolve to resist the cookies displayed significantly less willpower when asked to rely on it in a second exercise immediately following the cookie exercise.

Although the Heaths' book provides a much more detailed and thorough explanation of what it takes to change, the bottom line is fairly straightforward: Your willpower will grow weaker as you use it over the short term.

Of course, you didn't need a study conducted on college kids to know this. You likely discovered it on January 3, after you fell off the wagon from whatever New Year's resolution you made.

That's why success in life and business is not about the big commitments you *make* on New Year's Day; it's about the small commitments you *keep* every day of January, February, and every month after. You cannot rely on willpower and self-discipline alone to help you take the consistent actions you need, because they will fail you in critical moments of temptation. You need something to strengthen and support these actions—something to keep you going during those moments of weakness.

You need something to get you to make that sixth cold call *every day*—to change you at a fundamental level so that *doing* the right things on a consistent basis is not a constant battle.

What you need is to have your subconscious mind programmed to do what you need to do automatically. You need these actions to become second nature, just like your drive home from work. And you will get this from the strength of character and conviction that flows from your quiet-time ritual. You need to place new, second-nature actions into your box and be able to remove them at critical moments on your journey to wealth and success. You must develop a new approach deep within your subconscious mind that will keep you on track on a *consistent* basis—a guidepost that ensures your actions are consistent with what you want, what you want to become, and what you want to contribute in life and business.

You will get all that—*and more*—by investing 15 minutes a day into your quiet-time ritual.

This period of time is the well from which you will draw the strength you need to make the right decisions consistently. It's the cornerstone on which you will create the life and business of your dreams; it's what will keep you strong and unshakable on your journey. Your quiet-time ritual will program the life of your dreams at a core level so that you can develop the deep emotional commitment that never allows you to forget what you need to do. It will keep you on track on a subconscious level, no matter how distracted your conscious mind becomes. Your quiet-time ritual will strengthen and support your willpower and self-discipline.

As I stated in Chapter 5, the purpose of your quiet-time ritual is to program new thoughts and beliefs into your box that you will remove in moments of uncertainty and weakness. Eventually, your life will be a perfect reflection of the prosperity plan you placed in the box during your quiet-time rituals.

This time will also serve as a powerful daily guide for keeping you on track. As your subconscious mind is programmed to work toward your dreams by taking the consistent steps outlined in your prosperity plan, you will create a new level of personal accountability to yourself.

Stop for a moment and review your prosperity plan. Is there any doubt that if you performed your consistency actions *every day* that eventually you would reach your consistency outcomes? No, because we know that you simply can't do the right things and accidentally create the wrong results. Your quiet-time ritual's job is to ensure that you perform your consistency actions daily, thereby effectively guaranteeing a new level of success in your sales and business career.

For example, suppose your prosperity plan includes earning a six-figure income, and you have outlined in your consistency actions, "I make six new cold calls per day." You've already figured out, based on your sales model and performance, that six new calls per day will result in fairly reliable sales results, which will result in you achieving your desired income goals.

Now imagine you spend 15 minutes during your quiet-time ritual reviewing your personal prosperity plan and repeating your "I make six new cold calls per day" consistency action. You allow yourself to experience the emotions of what that six-figure income is going to mean to your family and your future. You allow yourself to feel as though it's already happened.

Now imagine that it's 4:00 PM that afternoon and you've made only four new cold calls.

What do you suppose is going to happen? Most likely you will feel like crawling out of your skin or feel like a fish out of water. You may hear alarm bells sounding in your head.

Compare that with the feeling you would have had after making four new cold calls if you *had not* programmed six new cold calls into your box. Without the quiet-time ritual, you likely would have been perfectly content to accept a four-call performance from yourself. It's the added pressure of those two additional calls that have led you to significantly raise your expectations for yourself. And, as you're aware, your expectations set the limits on your results. Raise your expectations, and the results will soon follow.

Because you have so deeply programmed yourself to take this action—*and* allowed yourself to experience the emotions of what will happen as a result of doing so—you aren't likely to let yourself off the hook after making only four calls.

This is why failing to make six calls will create internal conflict. You are not going to be able to ignore the fact that you didn't make the six calls. Your quiet-time ritual will have created a new standard of expectations for yourself, and if you don't rise to your new expectations, you won't be able to reconcile your expectations with your actions.

If you hadn't set this goal for yourself, you wouldn't experience any internal conflict when failing to do what you said you would. Since you never created the dream and allowed yourself to experience what it will feel like when you earn that six-figure income, you will effortlessly let yourself off the hook. Your results will never surpass your expectations—and you will remain comfortably in mediocrity.

This higher level of achievement and personal accountability is a reflection of the consistency principle that "private declarations dictate future actions." The bottom line is this: You are far more likely to do something if you have told yourself you are going to do it. If you don't bother making this kind of promise to yourself, there is nothing to which you must hold yourself accountable. And this lack of internal pressure allows you to let yourself off the hook.

You already know that your results are pretty much certain if you do the things you know you should do. If you do the right things, you can create only the right things. The only question is: Are you going to do them?

The consistency principle that "private declarations dictate future actions" capitalizes on a reality of human nature called cognitive dissonance. This is the anxiety or discomfort we feel when we hold conflicting ideas and beliefs. Therefore, if you tell yourself that you are going to do certain things during your quiet-time ritual and you believe that you will generate success by doing those things, you will experience cognitive dissonance if you fail to take actions that are consistent with your private declarations.

This may be a new level of personal accountability for you, but it is the kind of accountability that will drive you to new levels of sales and business success. By outlining your new life and business in your prosperity plan—and programming it into your box during your quiet-time ritual—you will leverage cognitive dissonance and drive yourself to unparalleled levels of personal accountability and success.

By creating and programming your prosperity plan deep into your subconscious during your quiet-time ritual, you will create a powerful new ally for your willpower and self-control. You will strengthen your personal resolve to do what you need to do to get what you want to get.

This is how a high-school dropout, broke, homeless, and thrice convicted loser, can walk out of the penitentiary to a homeless shelter and create $20 million in sales in 60 months—and then earn a spot on *Inc.* magazine's list of fastest-growing privately held companies in America. I simply created a prosperity plan, got deeply emotionally committed to that plan over seven years of quiet-time rituals, and then allowed cognitive dissonance to drive my actions that guaranteed wealth, happiness and peace of mind.

Hey, it's not rocket science. If a knucklehead like me with a 103 IQ can do it, then why can't you? You can and you *will*—if you follow this very predictable process.

The Power of Consistency relies on the human tendency to work to eliminate cognitive dissonance, in this case by taking the actions programmed during quiet-time rituals. Sadly, however, there is another way we humans can eliminate the anxiety of holding conflicting ideas and beliefs: by eliminating the expectations from our prosperity plan or abandoning the quiet-time ritual altogether. In other words, if we never create the expectation that we are going to do something, there will be no dissonance when we fail to do it. We let ourselves off the hook by *never* raising our expectations.

Suppose you have created your prosperity plan and programmed the consistency action into your subconscious mind that you will make six new calls per day. You go out on day 1 and make only one new call. The cognitive dissonance drives you to the verge of insanity! What happens next?

On day 2, you do your quiet-time ritual again and head out to work. After letting yourself settle for one call the day before and feeling terrible about it, your new level of personal accountability drives you to make the six calls. You do it again the next day, and the next.

The next thing you know, you are making six calls per day, and—like any new habit—it becomes easier after 25 to 30 days. Soon, *not* making the six calls is the exception. You are making the six calls consistently. What is the impact on your income? What result will you have created?

As long as you include making the six calls per day in your quiet-time ritual, you will find the internal strength to follow through. Once you regularly engage in the consistency actions, the consistency outcome is fairly predictable. Cognitive dissonance drives the new behavior, which drives the new results, and next thing you know you are a top income producer.

But suppose you took the easy way out and got rid of the cognitive dissonance by eliminating the quiet-time ritual on day 2 instead of making the six calls. You eradicate the anxiety in both cases—but with two very different long-term outcomes with respect to your business and income.

Creating your prosperity plan and programming it into your subconscious will force you to eliminate any cognitive dissonance by doing one of two things:

1. You will eventually *begin taking consistent actions* and creating better results.
2. You will *completely abandon* your quiet-time ritual.

You simply cannot have it both ways. Push will come to shove at some point.

Ask yourself how long you could review your dreams (and the things you need to do to reach them) each morning, and then fail to follow through during the course of your day. If you're like most people, then your answer is "probably not very long." Eventually, you would either have to quit dreaming or start acting in harmony with your prosperity plan. Human nature guarantees that you will eventually eliminate cognitive dissonance one way or another.

Failing to achieve your dreams in life and business would be regrettable, but lying to yourself would be far worse. If you create a prosperity plan and review it daily during your quiet-time ritual—yet you continue to live your life as if the plan did not exist—you would have become both con and mark. There is nothing worse that fooling ourselves.

At some point in life and business, we either have to give up and make excuses for failure and mediocrity, or we have to strive harder and hold ourselves accountable. Once you accept that better results are guaranteed by doing better things, the only reason for failure is a personal decision to fail.

That may sound harsh, but it's true. Failing to meet your goals is simply a result of not doing the right things on a consistent basis. If failure was the result of external forces—a weak economy, bad leads, cheap competitors, or a stupid boss—then everyone in a similar situation would have similar results. And that's just not the reality. There are successful sales and business professionals working right alongside losers. The only difference between the two is in what they think and what they do.

If you think and do the right things, wealth and success are simply a matter of when, not if. Nothing will hold you back or get in your way. You will create a new and better financial future for yourself and your family—because you simply cannot think and do the right things and accidentally create the wrong results. The universe doesn't work that way.

A few months ago, I went bowling for the first time in years. I was amazed at how easy it was to put the ball into the gutter, given how small the gutter was relative to the entire lane. I kept finding the gutter and then noticed a device that could be pulled down to block them.

I asked one of the bowling alley employees about the device. "Oh," she said, "those are bumpers that block the gutters. But they are only for the kids."

"Aw, come on," I said, "Let me try it just once."

"Okay," she responded, "But just *once!*"

I lowered the bumpers and let the ball fly. As it headed for the gutter it bounced off the bumper and careened across the lane to the other bumper. Back and forth it went from side to side as it worked its way down the lane, eventually taking out a few pins.

Your quiet-time ritual essentially puts bumpers on your daily actions. We're all human, so we're all going to fall short occasionally. But once you get emotionally committed to your dreams, you'll never stray very far off course. You may get close to the gutter and let yourself pass on making the number of calls you have committed to make, but your subconscious mind will kick in and remind you of your consistency actions.

It's a powerful mechanism for personal accountability. Programming what you want and what you need to do to achieve it in your quiet-time ritual will keep you on track no matter how distracted you become with life's daily tasks and disruptions.

I can't guarantee that you will follow this process and leverage *The Power of Consistency*. However, if I can get you to stick with it, it *will* forever keep you from settling for mediocrity. You'll never be the same once you know what's possible. You may not always do what you *need* to do, but you will know what you gave up on.

You have the talents, skills, and ability to create the sales and business results you desire. Now you have the know-how as well. If you don't follow through, you have no one to blame but yourself. It's okay if you don't; just be honest enough with yourself to admit that you chose not to. These are just the facts of life. Don't shoot the messenger.

I'd like to share one more brief example of how your prosperity plan and quiet-time ritual can keep you moving consistently toward your dreams.

Suppose your consistency outcome is "I weigh 180 pounds" and your consistency actions are "I eat only healthy and nutritional food" and "I exercise 30 minutes per day." Now imagine reviewing this each day and allowing yourself to visualize and experience what it's going to feel like when you have created the dream.

What do you suppose will happen if you find yourself eating delicious chocolate cake for lunch? Alarm bells will be blasting in your skull, and you'll feel incredibly disappointed in yourself. Ah, the power of cognitive dissonance.

If you continue the quiet-time ritual, your actions will eventually get in line with the dream. The only way they won't is if you quit your quiet-time ritual. Even if your actions aren't consistent with the dream initially, they will eventually get in alignment.

I have found out for myself, time and again, that programming your subconscious mind can—and *will*—move you closer to your dreams.

When I created my first prosperity plan after my father died in 1996, one of the things I wanted desperately to become was "a man of character, honor, and integrity." I reviewed my plan during my quiet-time ritual over the next several years and thought about what I needed to do to become that kind of man. I would allow myself to experience what it would feel like to be a man of character, honor, and integrity.

Obviously, I was a million miles away from being that person then. I was someone who had spent his entire adult life lying, cheating, and stealing. I was the antithesis of a man of character, honor, and integrity.

Nevertheless, I was determined to create a new reality for myself and achieve the dream of being trustworthy. So each day I would review my plan and ensure I was taking actions that were consistent with the dream. In prison, those actions were to stop playing the prison games. I could hardly tell myself "I am a man of honor, character, and integrity" each morning and then go out and smoke pot and drink "hooch" on the yard. It also meant that if I borrowed coffee or toothpaste until payday, I had to pay my debts as soon as possible without excuses. (By the way, paying debts in prison doubles as health insurance, because not paying them can be very bad for your health!)

Six years later, push came to shove, and I had to make a decision about whether or not I was going to act in a manner consistent with my dream. It was 2002—six years after my father died and just one year before I was released—when the time came to see what I was really all about.

One morning as I talked on the telephone, the cell house cop walked past me and suddenly collapsed to the cellblock floor. I quickly hung up the phone and rushed to join the crowd of convicts assembling around him as he suffered some type of seizure.

As I stood watching him convulse, he suddenly went completely still. Within seconds his face was grayish blue. It was obvious there was no oxygen going to his brain.

As I watched him die, I heard a voice in my head: "I am a man of character, honor, and integrity," something I had been telling myself every morning for six years. Suddenly cognitive dissonance kicked in as I watched this man struggle to maintain his tenuous grasp on life—and I knew I had to *do* something.

I was surprised by the internal voice—and I was suddenly aware that I had a choice. I was at a crossroads. I could either take actions consistent with being a man of character, honor, and integrity, or I could tuck my tail between my legs and return to my cell and scratch that dream off my list. I couldn't have it both ways; I couldn't be both con and mark.

And I wasn't about to scratch the dream off my list. I was moving ahead with my life, in a direction consistent with my dreams.

As I recounted in *The Upside of Fear*, I then took action consistent with my dream of becoming a better man and began what could only *remotely* be called CPR. Eventually I was assisted by a lieutenant who knew CPR and successfully revived officer Mark McClure.

I received a letter from the warden thanking me for my actions two weeks later. He said in his letter that I had demonstrated that I was a man of "good character."

Character. One of the exact words I had written on my prosperity plan many years earlier.

The lesson is simple: Outline the life and business of your dreams in your prosperity plan and program the dreams into your subconscious mind through your daily quiet-time ritual. Following these steps will program your consistency outcomes and consistency actions into your box, thereby giving you the strength and determination to take the actions necessary to make the dream a reality.

When push comes to shove, you will find yourself taking the actions you know you need to take. Once that happens, the results are certain because you can't do one thing and accidentally create something else. You will have solved the conundrum of human nature. You will know what you need to do to create wealth, happiness, and peace of mind—*and you will do it.*

One of the most remarkable things about the quiet-time ritual is you will find over time that it becomes less of a struggle to take actions consistent with your dreams. You will feel your emotional state changing as you begin feeling as though the parts of your prosperity plan are already a reality. You will approach each day with passion, purpose, and confidence.

When you start *thinking* like a success, you start *feeling* like a success. When you start *feeling* like a success, you start *acting* like a success. When you start *acting* like a success, you start *creating* successful results. And the next thing you know, you are living your dreams.

You will find that you make the right decisions on a more consistent basis as you follow this process. These choices will simply come more naturally, with less effort. As you change your thoughts and program your dreams into your subconscious, you will find your emotional state changes, making it easier to take the consistent actions toward your dreams.

It's all one big self-fulfilling prophecy. It isn't rocket science. It's just the way the universe works.

CHAPTER SEVEN

Step 4: Responsibility

Look at the word responsibility—"response-ability"—the ability to choose your response.

—Dr. Stephen R. Covey

Bad things happen to good people. That's the bad news.

But there's good news: Your results in life and business are far more likely to be a reflection of what you decide to do about the bad things that happen in your life than a reflection of the bad things themselves.

It is your responsibility alone to make good decisions when bad things happen in your life and business, because these good decisions will beget positive results. Ultimately, your life will be an accumulation of your decisions—for better or for worse.

Everyone faces problems in life—financial, health, relationship, work—just insert your problem here and you'll see what I mean. Every sales and business professional on the planet has to deal with a weak economy, customers with bad credit, lower-priced competitors, and company operations units that seem determined to undermine every sale you make.

Get over it. Succeed in the face of it. Kick its ass. Whatever you do, don't just lie down and use those things as excuses for failure. It doesn't matter how bad things are at your company or in your market; countless businesspeople are succeeding right now under the same conditions. Some of them may be sitting in the room with you at this very moment.

What's the difference between the two groups of people? I can tell you this: It is not in what they *know*. The highest earners don't know anything the lowest earners don't know. But one thing is for sure: The top producers are *doing* a few things that the losers won't do.

Dr. M. Scott Peck began his landmark book, *The Road Less Travelled*, with the simple truth that "Life is difficult." Everybody has challenges along the way. Nobody gets out of this deal alive.

The question is not whether you are going to face any obstacles in life and business; the question is, What are you going to do about it? Your *decisions*—not the amount or degree of problems—determine the outcome.

When I was running amok and acting as a complete menace to society (and ending up in prison as a result), I used to think that it was because I had really bad luck. I always thought, "If I could just catch a lucky break, things would be fine." It never occurred to me that I was creating my own luck with the decisions I was making in my life.

I can remember being at the mall around Christmastime after I had been to prison (and let out) for the first time. I saw a guy walking around with his pretty wife and his cute little kids. They were all smiles and giggles, and I just knew they had a nice little house with a white picket fence and puppies.

I remember thinking, "That guy wouldn't be so damn happy if he had my problems and my luck. If he had to walk a mile in my shoes, he would know what it's like to suffer." It was all I could do not to walk over and wipe that smile off his face.

That's how bitter, jealous, pathetic, and miserable I was at that point in my life.

However, I learned later in life that the guy in the mall had problems too. Odds are that at some point in his life, he struggled with money, relationships, or his health.

The difference between the two of us was not in the nature of our problems. It was in the way we chose to handle our problems.

I'd be willing to bet that when that fellow had money problems, he decided to get a second job, work overtime, or reduce his expenses. When I had money problems, I decided to grab a gun and a ski mask. That was the only difference between us. My life was a pathetic mess because of what I decided do about my money problems. It was not the money problem itself.

Our decisions—whether good or bad—are 100 percent our responsibility (Figure 7.1).

Think about your box again and look at Figure 7.1. Some problem rears its ugly head in your life and business, and it goes into your box (your mind), where you make a decision about how to handle it. The situation's eventual outcome will be a reflection of your decision about this particular challenge. You can have a really bad problem come into your life and business, but if you make a good decision, you will most likely have a good outcome (Figure 7.2).

Let's say that you have two people facing identical circumstances; chances are, they'll make very different decisions about

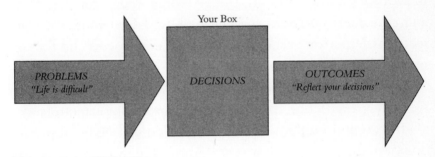

Figure 7.1   Your Box

Problems go in your box, and depending on what's in your box, you make a certain decision. Your decision will determine the outcome. Your decisions are 100 percent your RESPONSIBILITY.

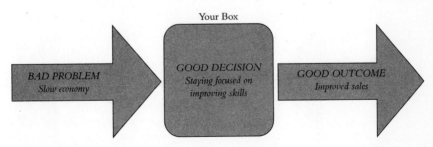

Figure 7.2

You can have a BAD PROBLEM come into your life and business, yet if you make a GOOD DECISION, you will likely create a GOOD OUTCOME. The OUTCOME is a reflection of the DECISION—not the problem.

how to handle the problem. The choice each one makes depends on what's in his or her box—and everybody's box is different. Take, for example, two sales professionals working in the same market. Both are facing the same problems: a slow economy, customers obsessed with a cheap price, and competition all too willing to give it.

Yet one sales professional consistently outperforms the other. Are their individual performances a reflection of the problem? Of course not—the problems are identical. Each person's sales performance reflects how he or she handles the issues. One decides to stay focused on improving skills and solving problems for clients, while the other decides that there is really no point in working hard. After all, the economy keeps getting worse and customers just want the cheapest available product. So the second salesperson rushes through the sales process and focuses on matching the competitor's low price.

Each sales professional's circumstances are identical. Their results are merely a reflection the way they approach their circumstances.

British philosophical writer James Allen said, "Circumstances do not make the man, they reveal him." The way in which you choose to handle your circumstances will reveal what kind of person you are.

Figure 7.3

You can have a GOOD PROBLEM come into your life and business, yet if you make a BAD DECISION, you will likely create a BAD OUTCOME. The OUTCOME is a reflection of the DECISION.

When you understand that the only thing between you and success is making better decisions, you are *empowered*. You are responsible. And you are capable of changing the course of your financial destiny—*immediately*. If you are waiting for the economy and your customers to get better before you start making more money, you may be broke for a while. But if you realize that you don't have to *wait* for anything to become prosperous—you just need to make better decisions—then you can immediately take charge of your sales and business career. You should welcome this reality and embrace the opportunity to take responsibility for your decisions and the quality of your life.

Whatever your life and career currently look like, you have to analyze your decisions to figure out how you created them and to decide if you want to change them. It may be tempting—and downright easy—to blame your problems on a particular situation, but we know that this usually isn't the case. Often, when we struggle in our lives and business, we blame others or circumstances for our problems rather than taking responsibility for our decisions and the problems that resulted from them. In the context of *The Power of Consistency*, this is all about taking responsibility for your decisions in life and business and being accountable for what's in your box, because that's where all your decisions originate.

By the way, the opposite of Figure 7.2 is also true (see Figure 7.3). Sometimes we can have a good problem but make bad a decision. In this situation, the outcome will predictably reflect the bad decision as well, not the good problem. Ever heard of the lottery curse? Winning the lottery is a good problem to have, but how often do we hear stories of lottery winners making bad decisions about their winnings? Is the ultimate outcome a reflection of the good problem or the bad decision? The bad decision, of course. Our ultimate outcomes are typically a reflection of our decisions—for better or for worse.

I remember the liberation and freedom I felt—even while in prison—when I realized my life was a reflection of my decisions, and *I alone* was therefore responsible for my life's quality and circumstances. This realization set me free. I understood for the first time that because I created my disastrous results in life by making bad decisions, I could *improve* my life by making good decisions—and I knew I could change things.

Think about your life through this lens. If the nature of the problems that come your way must change before your life gets better, what are the odds that your luck is going to change anytime soon? The truth is that you don't need better luck. You need to make better decisions. And programming better things into your box by using the FEAR process virtually guarantees that you'll make them—which in itself virtually guarantees better results. And that's all you need to start improving your life.

How often, throughout the course of your day, do you really have to *think about* the decisions you make? Most of us live our lives on autopilot. We never have to think very hard. We get up, eat breakfast, take the kids to school, go to work, interact with coworkers, deal with customers, return some e-mails and calls, go home, watch *American Idol*, take a shower, and go to bed. Then rinse and repeat.

Whether you realize it or not, you are making a thousand instantaneous (second nature) decisions throughout your day. If you aren't thinking about those countless decisions consciously, where are they coming from?

You guessed it: They are coming from your subconscious box. You reach into your box and pull out automatic decisions a thousand times a day. Your life is a perfect reflection of what's in your box. You are pulling out its contents every single day. That's why you had better know what's in there—the nature of your decisions determines the nature of your life and business. Once you take responsibility for programming what's in your box, you are holding yourself accountable for your decisions. By putting a life of abundance, wealth, and prosperity—and the consistency actions necessary to get there—into your box, you are setting yourself up to eventually pull those things out of your box. If you make a deliberate effort to put what you want in there, rather than allowing other people to fill it with their stuff, you create and achieve your dreams.

Your box will always be full of something. The question is whether this happens by design or default. It's up to you.

Remember: Life is difficult. So is business. So is sales. Be prepared to make good decisions if you want to transcend those difficulties and create wealth, happiness, and peace of mind in both.

Where Your Thoughts Go, Your Actions Go; Where Your Actions Go, Your Results Go

Another facet of this is taking responsibility for where we focus our thoughts.

Winners think about the things they can *control*—namely, their own sales performance. Whiners, on the hands, obsess over matters over which they have no control, such as the economy, competitors offering cheaper prices, and their bosses.

Winners think about how they can improve their sales, relationship building, product knowledge, and closing skills. Whiners think about how others should be doing their jobs better.

Winners focus on "I"; whiners focus on "they."

You can basically break down everything in sales and business development into two basic categories: *process* and *result*.

The process includes all the activities that define your sales activities: building relationships, identifying problems and offering solutions for your clients, demonstrating how and why your product and service are superior, and creating and delivering a powerful and effective closing sequence. It also includes the amount of time and effort you invest into learning and mastering the sales profession and how well you prepare yourself by reading and role-playing.

The *result* is simple: whether or not your prospect buys.

Here's the rub: You have 100 percent control over the *processes* involved in sales and 0 percent control over the results. Now here's the rub-a-dub-dub: Many sales and business professionals spend very little time thinking about the process and spend *beaucoup* time obsessing over whether or not someone is going to buy from them. In other words, they obsess over that which they have no control and ignore the part over which they have *total* control.

Now, I'm not saying that you can't have *influence* over whether or not your prospect buys from you. You can dramatically sway prospects to buy from you by how well you perform the sales process. The better you are at your profession, the more likely your prospects are to buy from you. You can *influence* that decision; however, you can't *control* it. You will not ultimately be making that decision for them. You can only make *your* decisions.

Your income and sales success will grow in direct proportion to the amount of time you spend focusing your thoughts and energy on the part of sales you control: building relationships, solving problems for your prospects, and closing. Focus on what you control and watch your income grow.

The more you focus on what you cannot control—the result—the more you will be dependent on luck and lay-downs to make your living.

Again, I'm not saying that you don't plan for and visualize successful sales outcomes. You must do those things. I am saying that when it comes time to get down in the trenches and actually run a sales call, you must be highly skilled and prepared.

You must concentrate on elements such as your skill level, confidence, and attitude.

In his landmark best seller, *The 7 Habits of Highly Effective People*, the late Dr. Stephen R. Covey discussed the effectiveness of focusing on your circle of influence versus your circle of concern. Your circle of influence includes the areas of your life and business that you can do something about, such as processes you control during a sales call. Your circle of concern includes areas of your life and business that you are concerned about but have no ability to control, such as the economy or your competition.

Dr. Covey explains how proactive (or effective) people tend to focus on their circle of influence, whereas reactive (ineffective) people tend to focus on their circle of concern—things they are concerned about but over which they have no control. Focusing on things we can't control is a loser's game.

Be a winner. Not a whiner.

Prepare Yourself for Success

In addition to taking responsibility for your decisions, you must also take responsibility for your success. It sounds like that would be easy, but it sometimes takes more effort than you might think. It's especially difficult if your box is full of limiting beliefs that have festered for many years.

Everyone has what is called homeostasis. Really smart people have fancy ways to define homeostasis. However, I am not one of those people, so I define it as our *comfort zone*.

Your homeostasis is what makes you uniquely *you*—your job, your income, your spouse, your home, and what you like for dessert. It's everything in your life that makes you happy. If you think about your life as a thermometer, your homeostasis is your perfect temperature. It's where you feel "just right."

Imagine your comfort zone is a perfect 70 degrees, but something comes along in life to lower your temperature, knocking you out of your comfort zone. For example, sometimes people get divorced, lose their jobs, or lose their homes in foreclosure. After all, bad things sometimes happen to good people, right?

But this is what I love about human nature: When something comes along and knocks us out of our comfort zone, we *do something about it!* Most of us won't just sit there and wallow in misery. We get up, dust ourselves off, and do what we have to do get back to homeostasis. The "lower temperature" doesn't feel comfortable, so we take action to get things back on track.

We find a new job or rent a new place to live. We start dating or even get remarried. The bottom line is that when we get knocked out of our homeostasis, we take some kind of action to regain our balance and fix it. We don't just lie there and take it. We work hard and fight our way back. It's an awesome, admirable characteristic of human nature.

Of course, sometimes a life event occurs that *raises* our temperature—in other words, makes things better. And here's the kicker: Often, these positive events can feel *just as uncomfortable* as the negative ones!

It sounds a little crazy, and tough to imagine, but sometimes success can make us uncomfortable because we are not used to it. It doesn't feel "normal" to us. We can become so comfortable with the way our lives are that we perceive *anything* that challenges our homeostasis as a threat, even if it holds the potential to improve our lives.

When this happens, it is not inconceivable that we will sabotage our success and self-destruct. Have you ever known someone who endures difficult periods and occasionally seems to start to improve, only to self-destruct again? To that person, success might feel just as uncomfortable as failure.

I must confess that there have been times as my life has rocketed toward success when I found myself feeling a little uneasy. It sounds a little insane, but after spending 20 years in a state of despair and misery, I got comfortable there. It reached a point where prison and poverty seemed like the norm.

There have been times where I shared the stage with Dr. Stephen R. Covey or the legendary Tom Hopkins and found myself looking out over the audience and thinking, "Who am I kidding? Do I really belong here?"

I remember once having dinner at Mala Ocean Tavern on Maui next to Mick Fleetwood and thinking to myself, "Dude, you have no business being here. Who do you think you are?" Success and prosperity can take some getting used to, especially when all you've ever known is struggle.

To counter the potential of doing something that may undermine our success, we must take responsibility for getting comfortable with success. Understand the fact that you may have subtly undermined success because it didn't feel comfortable. Be aware of the human tendency to avoid discomfort *even if it has the potential to improve your life and business.*

Once you understand this phenomenon, you can simply add a new consistency outcome to your quiet-time ritual to ensure you are comfortable with new levels of prosperity. Adding something like "I deserve unlimited abundance and prosperity" or "I am comfortable with wealth and success" will help you condition yourself for the great things that are to come.

The bottom line is that success will breed more success—and you need to make sure you are comfortable when it happens.

Values, Character, and Integrity

Your values, character, and integrity will affect your level of success in life and business—and all three are your responsibility.

One of my favorite sayings is "Time will expose you or pro-mote you." You can fool some of the people some of the time, but eventually your values, character, and integrity will bubble to the surface.

Dr. Stephen R. Covey provides one of the best discussions on this topic in *The 7 Habits*. He points out the difference between values and principles, noting that whereas values are subjective, principles are timeless and universal. Criminals have common values, but those values may not result in long-term success and prosperity. Thus, when I refer to "values," I am referring to timeless and universal standards of conduct.

When I began reading about these standards of conduct, I was overwhelmed by how I had been living my life. I was, at the time, a career criminal who'd spent my adult life lying, cheating, and stealing. Nevertheless, after reading *The 7 Habits*, I realized success would never find me in the forest of my dishonesty and dysfunction.

David Starr Jordan, educator and founding president of Stanford University, wrote, "There is no excellence in all the world that can be separated from right living." After I exam-ined the poverty and struggle that governed my life for many years—and compared that to my life of abundance and prosper-ity today—it's easy to see how my values, character, and integ-rity played into each.

I synthesized what I learned this way in *The Upside of Fear:* "Values are knowing what to do. Character is having the strength to do it. And Integrity is doing it when no one is watching."

Values

As you begin the process of designing and implementing your personal prosperity plan, be sure that the values that govern your life and business align with the universal principles as dis-cussed in *The 7 Habits* and other places. Consider how you will handle your affairs. What values will govern your behavior in life and business?

When I started a little heating and air-conditioning company in my living room in 2004, we offered our customers an unconditional "One Year Test Drive." This meant that customers could hire our company to install a system and have it removed anytime during the first year after installation for a 100 percent refund.

This "risk reversal" guarantee was put to the test during our first two years in business. On one occasion we honored the guarantee when a homeowner got sick, lost her job, and needed the system removed. We allowed her to keep the system (which she needed) and refunded a significant portion of her investment.

There were other instances where our company made mistakes and always assumed financial responsibility for the problem. I once made a design mistake and had to pay for costly electrical work to make the system work properly. Many companies would have told the homeowner, "This wasn't our problem. We aren't responsible for the electrical capacity in your home." But that wasn't how our company operated. I knew it was *my* mistake, and I took the hit on it. It was the right thing to do.

As time unfolded and both our customers and employees learned that we were serious about serving our customers at this level, we grew very rapidly—to $20 million in revenue in 60 months. As mentioned previously, we also earned a spot on *Inc.* magazine's list of fastest-growing privately held companies in America.

By staying true to the values we outlined for our company, we were rewarded with our community's business—and trust.

Character

Character means having the strength to stay true to those values, even when it's tough—in fact, *especially* when it's tough. I once had a salesmen named Winston Dennis who consistently outperformed all other salesmen. He consistently produced sales well in excess of $1 million in an industry where $1 million in sales is the Holy Grail.

One day Winston approached me with a proposal: increase his bonus points on revenue if he hit *$2 million* in annual sales. I agreed, thinking he would increase his sales but never expecting him to actually hit $2 million.

He did it. And he did it for the *next three consecutive years*, which cost me tens of thousands of dollars in bonus commissions. But I gave him my word and had to muster the strength of character to honor my word, no matter how much it cost me.

We must be bound by our word to succeed in life and business. Whether it's a promise we make to a customer, a supplier, or an employee, our word must always mean *something*. If we make commitments and promises and then waffle when push comes to shove, it's only a matter of time before we are exposed—and our business suffers as a consequence.

Integrity

Integrity means doing all that great stuff when no one is watching. Several years ago, my son, Hunter, and I were riding dirt bikes in the hills of Colorado's Western Slope. After a day of riding, we checked into a hotel for a night's rest. We pulled into the hotel parking lot in my full-size pickup, pulling a long motorcycle trailer. Because the rig was so long, it was hard to maneuver through tight spots.

I parked way out at the edge of the parking lot where it was empty so that I wouldn't have to squeeze into a tight spot. The next morning my son and I walked out to the parking lot to find it jam packed with cars. Our truck and trailer were sardined in between cars on all sides.

Hunter was only about 12 years old, but he did his best to guide me as I tried to work the rig out of the tight space without hitting other cars. I would back out a few feet, pull up, and try to get a better angle. We were making progress little by little, an inch at a time, but finally I cut it too close and the trailer etched a nice scar into the side of a parked car.

Eventually, we extricated the truck and trailer from the other cars. I parked the rig and walked over to the car I had engraved with the trailer. It was an old, beat-up car. It was actually in such bad shape that it was hard to tell where I gouged it.

I took out a business card, wrote a note to the owner, and placed it under the windshield wiper. As I walked back to the truck, a little old lady who had been watching the whole fiasco from the secrecy of her car stepped out to congratulate me for leaving the note. It felt really good getting "caught" doing something right—and even better that my son was there and learned such a great lesson.

A few days later I got a call from the kid who owned the car. After I apologized, he said, "To be honest, I couldn't really tell where you hit it. Not sure if you noticed, but the car is a bit of a mutt."

I explained that I didn't think the car's condition was the issue, and I wanted to fix it. He told me that was unnecessary, but he appreciated the offer. As we talked I learned he was in college. I asked him if I could at least take care of his rent for a month. After a moment of silence, he said, "Actually, *that* would be great!"

I sent the kid a few hundred bucks to help out. I felt really good again—this time, about doing the right thing when *no one* was watching.

Consequences for our actions, for better or for worse, will eventually pay us a visit. The values, character, and integrity that govern your life and business will have a significant impact on your wealth and prosperity. They are inextricable.

I once heard a great saying: "You can't talk yourself out of a situation that you acted your way into." To create the levels of wealth, happiness, and prosperity of which we are capable, we must accept responsibility for where we are today—and how we got there.

Years ago, I read a book that outlined a simple acronym that I have found very useful in my life and business: CPA. This means that I *cause, permit, or allow* everything that happens in my life. I am never a victim or at the mercy of anything or anyone.

Now I can hear the protests coming my way as some folks lament, "Some of the things that have happened in my life are *not* my fault! They are completely out of my control!"

To a degree, you are right. There are occasions when things happen in your life that are truly out of your control. But I would personally rather take the chance of assuming responsibility for something out of my control than bear the consequences of *not* taking responsibility for something *within* my control.

Because as long as I take responsibility for something, I can make it better and improve the situation. So what if I improve a situation that was somebody else's responsibility? I am creating results! I am not willing to ignore something just because it is technically "someone else's job"; I am going to make the situation better if I can. Don't get me wrong; whoever ignores their responsibility will hear from me loud and clear. But I am going to focus on improving things first.

In the immortal words of Dr. Stephen R. Covey: "Be a light, not a judge." Help others. Help yourself. And help improve the situation where you can. Don't look for blame; look for the opportunity to make a positive difference in life and business. And do it because you can—not because you must.

Think about what goes in your box and how what's in there affects your decisions. Prepare yourself to expect success. Consider what values, character, and integrity will define your life and business. And accept total responsibility for the results you enjoy.

Eight to Be Great!

I have one final thought regarding personal responsibility with respect to being a successful professional salesperson.

Think about the characteristics of your perfect prospect. How is that person's credit? Does he or she have a strong need for your product or service? Does the prospect have an unlimited budget? Is he or she loyal to your company?

As you consider the perfect prospect, write out eight characteristics that describe that person. Next to that list, write out eight characteristics of the perfect *you*—the perfect sales professional. (See Table 7.1.)

Now consider this: You only need *any* combination of eight to be great in sales. In other words, if your prospect is a perfect eight, you can be a below average sales professional and still be very successful. But if your prospect is a two or three, you must be a five or six if you expect to succeed. In most cases your prospect will have only a few of the perfect characteristics, so you will need to make up the difference. The wonderful news is that even if your prospects are "zeros," you can still be very successful in sales if you are an eight. Get the picture? So instead

Table 7.1 Eight to Be Great!

Perfect Prospect	Perfect You
Good credit	Highly motivated
Honest	Well trained
Loyal	Persistent
High need	Focused
Unlimited budget	Confident
Values quality	Expert communicator
Values service	Fearless
Willing to listen	High product knowledge

of complaining about the economy or your prospect, the key to sales success is focusing on *you* and improving your skill set, your attitude, and the contents of your box.

After all, how much control do you have over whether your prospect is a two or an eight? How much control do you have over being the perfect sales professional?

The truth is that you have 0 percent control over your prospects' level of need and financial condition; however, you have 100 percent control over *you*. So where are you going to spend your mind's energy? Are you going to fret and complain about economic and prospect characteristics over which you have no control? Or are you going to spend your precious time and energy working on making yourself the very best you can be, something over which you have total control?

You see it's not just *how* you think; it's *what you are thinking about*. Where's your focus? As I've mentioned about 1,000 times, your life is a reflection of what's in your box—and your box is a reflection of the things you focus on. You can focus on things you can't control (which will change nothing), or you can focus on the things you can control (which can change everything).

At the end of the day, we must assume responsibility for what is in our boxes and where we focus our energy and attention. Focus on programming your box with what you want out of your career and life and never forget that your circumstances will not define you. Only your decisions will do that.

Listen closely to others' conversations during your next sales meeting. Bottom-feeders typically complain about things beyond their control. Top producers stay focused on improving themselves and the elements of the sales process they can influence.

If you can't control your prospects, why spend time worrying about them? Just be the very best you can be, and your talents and professionalism will bridge the gap with mediocre prospects. And imagine the business you will write when you are an eight and your prospect is a five! It will be like shooting fish in a barrel (with a really big gun and a really small barrel).

One of the keys to being a top producer in sales is knowing how to think and what to think about. The more you know about what's in your box—and the more effort you expend putting what you want in there and remaining focused on things you control—the more success you will see in your sales career.

That's what *The Power of Consistency* is all about. To succeed, you must program your mind to prosper in the face of any obstacle and to overcome any challenge, including imperfect prospects. When you do that, nothing will hold you back or keep you down.

Take the time to identify what you want in life, what you want to become, and what you want to contribute. Write those things out in present tense and review them for 15 minutes during your quiet-time ritual. Allow yourself to experience the emotion as if you have already achieved your dreams and commit yourself to taking actions that are congruent with your personal prosperity plan. Take responsibility for your decisions in life and business, knowing that your life is a reflection of your decisions, not your problems. And keep your focus on the things in life you can control, which in most cases is *only you*.

After creating your prosperity mindset and spending a few minutes each day programming your box with wealth, success, and prosperity, you will become a top producer in the world of sales and business.

CHAPTER EIGHT

It's Not a Knowledge Problem; It's a Consistency Problem!

We are what we repeatedly do. Excellence, therefore, is not an act, but a habit.

—Aristotle

I read somewhere that only about 10 percent of people who start a book actually finish it. So if you have made it this far—congratulations! That's a pretty good sign that you really want success and are willing to do the work necessary.

If we hopped out of bed every morning, reviewed our business and personal goals for 15 minutes, ate a healthy breakfast, ran 3 miles, executed our responsibilities perfectly in our sales career, and made the projected number of cold calls every single day, life would be perfect. *We* would be perfect. We would be Stepford People.

But we aren't perfect—that's just not real life. Real life is a lot more complicated.

We all know what we *should* do all the time. Human nature, however, is somewhat fickle. And despite our best efforts, our actions don't always align perfectly with what we know we should do.

Nothing you have read in this book is going to make an ounce of difference unless you actually *do something* with the information. You have to figure out a way to implement what you've learned throughout these pages.

The implementation step is by far the most important step in your life and business—there is nothing I can write that will take the place of action on your part. There is, indeed, a lot to do, but a million words on the subject will not magically result in the doing. No amount of saying or reading is going to replace the value in the simple act of doing. There is no substitute for taking action.

Remember: The most successful people in life and business don't know anything the rest of us don't know. They are just doing things many others don't do.

Emerson wrote that "our actions speak so loudly others can't hear what we say." All I can say to that is "Amen."

Success in life and business is based on probabilities, not absolutes. There are no guarantees. Our best shot for success rests on our ability to do the little things in life, as often as we can, that will improve our chances for success.

The implementation conundrum draws on much of what we discussed in the first section of this book. Developing and reviewing your prosperity plan on a daily basis are two of the things that will dramatically improve your probabilities for success.

This is a reflection of the consistency principle, in that our "private affirmations dictate our future actions." In other words, it only makes sense that if we tell ourselves repeatedly that we are going to do something, we are *more likely* to do it. And even though "more likely" is an issue of probability, probability is all we have.

Common sense dictates that if you map out a specific plan for your life and business (prosperity plan) and keep it in the forefront of your consciousness by reviewing it every day (quiet-time ritual), you will be *more likely* to do those things than if you had not mapped them out and reviewed a plan. This daily review is like a "bumper" in a bowling alley—keeping those things prominent in your thinking and stopping you from hitting the gutter. And you know that if you take any action that is incongruent with your plan, you are *more likely* to feel cognitive dissonance and either correct—or at least not repeat—the action the next day.

At some point, you are *likely* to start acting in a manner congruent with your plan or stop reviewing the plan on a daily basis—since *telling* yourself one thing every morning and *doing* something very different over the course of your day will make you crazy.

But if you eventually begin *doing* the things you are *telling* yourself to do every day, you are *very likely* to achieve the result you desired when you initially wrote out the plan.

It's not rocket science.

Emerson said, "Mapping out a course of action and following it to an end takes courage." Many people have dreams of success and prosperity, but very few actually have the courage to map out the plan and follow it *to the end*. Reviewing it regularly will increase the probability that you will succeed, so be fearless. Be courageous.

The real challenge to implementing your plan is taking the time to conduct your quiet-time ritual every day. Once you cross that hurdle, you will become infinitely more likely to defy the conundrum of human nature and do the things you know you should do to create wealth, happiness, and peace of mind. Your quiet-time ritual will strengthen your willpower and assist you throughout the course of your day to act in a manner consistent with what you want in life and business.

Unfortunately, there is nothing that will help you make the quiet-time ritual a routine part of your life except actually *forcing* yourself to do it. This will require a fierce determination to succeed—and the discipline to do it. Whether that requires you to awaken 15 minutes earlier, do it over your lunch break, or stay up 15 minutes later at night, you will have to force yourself in the initial stages.

You've probably heard somewhere that it takes about 21–28 days for an action to become a habit. That means if you can force yourself to get through the first three weeks of doing your quiet-time ritual, you will be *dramatically more likely* to continue doing it thereafter.

Perhaps that's why Emerson said, "Mapping out a plan and following it to an end requires courage." If it were easy, sissies would do it.

The really good news is that it will become easier and more natural to do your quiet-time ritual over time. In fact, after a few days of doing it, you will likely find that it is the most amazing part of your day. You will find that this time brings a new sense of optimism and excitement into your life. As difficult as it may be to get started, it will be equally difficult to stop as you encounter the new hope and optimism about your life and business that will emanate from your 15-minute quiet-time ritual.

Two things can be especially helpful as you begin making your quiet-time ritual a habit: belief and understanding.

I can clearly remember beginning the process of reviewing my plan daily as I sat alone in a cold, gray prison cell. I considered whether or not it was worth the effort, and whether I truly believed it would make a difference in my life. As I was reflecting on this, I thought about something. Either my mind's ability to imagine amazing visions and dream astounding things serves a purpose—like everything else in my body—or it doesn't. And if it doesn't, then it is the *one* function of my body that serves no purpose. That would mean that it was there only to frustrate me with visions of things I could never have—to torment me with dreams I'll never achieve.

I honestly don't think that's how it is. I believe we have the ability to see wonderful, amazing things in our mind's eye because that is the first step on our journey to creating them. As Dr. Stephen R. Covey said: "All things are created twice," first in our mind, and again in our physical lives—that is, once in the box and once outside the box.

If you can believe that your quiet-time ritual serves a purpose, then it's much easier to get started on it. Once you understand the connection between your thoughts, emotions, actions, and results—and realize the important role that this time with yourself plays in that process—you will be more likely to make the adjustments necessary to take this decisive action. Once you take that decisive action, you will see dramatic changes in your attitude, actions, and results.

I think it is also useful to understand why it takes a few weeks for a new action to become a habit. If you understand the neurological process that is taking place over this course of making something a habit, you will be more likely to follow through with your attempts.

I first read about an amazing study that illustrates why it takes several weeks to form a habit in John Assaraf's best-selling book, *The Answer*. Assaraf details a NASA study whereby astronauts were fitted with lenses that inverted their vision 180 degrees. After approximately 25 days, one of the astronauts reported that his vision had automatically corrected itself and reinverted his sight 180 degrees. All of the astronauts in the study reported the same phenomenon within a few days. When the astronauts removed the lenses, their vision was again inverted 180 degrees.

The scientist discovered that after 25 to 30 days, the subjects' brains actually created new neural pathways to adjust for the inverted vision. A subsequent study also reported that researchers found that when the lenses were removed for 24 hours halfway through the study, subjects were essentially put back to square one. In other words, they had to start the 25 to 30 days from scratch.

The implication of this study is that the brain will adjust to make this new activity the "new normal" after performing an action for 25 to 30 days. This is why it is so critical to discipline yourself to do your quiet-time ritual for a few weeks so it seems routine—and why skipping even *one* day will require you to start from scratch. You need to perform the new action for 25 to 30 *consecutive* days in order to make the change permanent and habitual.

Change is *difficult*; there's no denying it. And human beings' tendency to resist it is legendary. We've all had the desire to change something, but after an initial push, things often revert to the path of least resistance.

Keeping the faith in your quiet-time ritual and putting in consistent effort—and understanding why it takes a little time to condition your brain for change—may help you break the gravitational pull of your old routine and ways of doing things.

It's also a good idea to place your prosperity plan in locations where you're sure to see it every day. Put it on your bathroom mirror so you see it first thing in the morning. Tape it to your coffee maker. Program it as a daily reminder on your smart phone. Stick it to your cell wall with toothpaste. Just put it somewhere so you can't miss it.

The constant reminder of its presence may influence you to take a few minutes to review it. But even that action of taking the time will require action to do it. In other words—there's no substitute for taking action.

The need for consistent implementation was the driving force behind ProsperityTV, which is a live, weekly interactive coaching show we stream on the Internet. When I first began training others to improve their sales and business performances, I often became frustrated by the lack of execution and implementation. Clients would be bouncing off the walls with energy and enthusiasm about taking their sales performance to new levels. But not even a month later, they'd be right back where they started. I created ProsperityTV to be the bridge between desire and action. It's the missing link in many sales programs. It's the answer to the conundrum of human nature.

Getting excited about new ideas and new ways of selling is a crucial preliminary step to changing your sales results. Ultimately, however, this initial excitement will fade. Before you know it, people are shelving all the new ideas in favor of what's comfortable, even if that means settling for mediocre sales results.

I knew I needed to do something to help clients move from this initial enthusiasm to actually *implementing and generating* sustainable improvements in sales performance. So I began hosting weekly live Internet shows to help motivate and focus clients every week. As we improved the shows, we began to see a corresponding long-term improvement in sales performance.

Today, we have a state-of-the-art studio and broadcast technology to connect with our clients weekly. We began doing the shows on Mondays with the intent of getting the week off to a positive start. We have added a call-in feature that allows me to take calls and answer questions on the air, as well as conduct live role-plays of particular sales scenarios or objections.

I believe active participation in the ongoing training and coaching is a critical component to sales success. Sometime a professional sales career can be daunting. Occasionally, we are distracted from our primary focus by the ins and outs of life. Sometime we get our teeth kicked in. And helping your navigate the challenges is what ProsperityTV on Monday mornings is all about. It's *my* responsibility to get you focused and excited about your career—and to help keep you on track. You can learn about this weekly coaching at www.WeldonLong.com.

There will be times on your journey to wealth and success when you feel overwhelmed, or even as though you can't consistently implement a new way of thinking. You may feel like it just isn't worth the effort.

But ask yourself one simple question during these moments of doubt and uncertainty: "How badly do I want it?" Do you want it just a little bit, willing to do the work if it's not *too* much of a pain in the ass? Or do you want it more that you've ever wanted anything in your life, and you are going to do whatever you have to do to reach your dreams? *That's* how bad you have to want it.

In January 2003, at 39 years of age, I walked out of the penitentiary for the last time. I was released to a halfway house in

Colorado Springs with nothing but a "box" full of wealth and success. I knew it was going to be a lot of work to start building a life from scratch with no job or work history and a record of 13 years behind the walls. I knew there would be no red carpet or celebration for me. It was up to *me* to take what I had learned and begin the process of building my new life.

My grandmother passed away just before my release, and she left me a few thousand dollars. I took that money and paid off my tuition to Southern California University for Professional Studies, where I had been taking classes for many years. By the time I walked out of the joint, I had earned a BS in law and a Management MBA. I had also spent years studying and mastering the sales process.

After paying off my tuition and receiving my degrees, I had enough money left over for a couple of suits and a pass to ride the transit line. My desire to get a job was strong. Through seven years of writing letters, I had maintained a relationship with my 10-year-old son, and a job would make it possible for me to get a place to live with my little boy.

So with a couple of jail house degrees, two suits, a bus pass, no work history or experience, and a felony record that spanned 15 years, I walked out the front door of the halfway house to build my fortune.

By all outward appearances, I must have looked silly—a wayward convict walking to the bus stop wearing an ill-fitted suit and holding an empty briefcase. But my mind was not empty at all. I had spent seven years filling it with homes and wealth, a relationship with my son, and a life of honor and integrity. I was convinced that if I took actions consistent with the contents of my box that eventually that life would come out.

I began looking for work. Each day I would walk into offices all over town with my elevator pitch: "Hi, I'm Weldon Long. I just need one opportunity. One shot. Give me a chance, and I'll sell more of whatever you sell than anyone ever has. I'll never cheat or lie. I'll never complain about the economy or the leads. I just need a chance."

My prospective employer would hear that and say, "Well, we need more attitudes like that around here. Tell me more!"

Then I would have to say, "Well, there is a little more to the story. I spent 13 years in prison and right now I live in a halfway house . . ." And that's when I would lose them.

"We appreciate you stopping in, but we aren't hiring right now," they would say.

"But you had an ad in the paper," I would plead.

"Oh yeah, but we filled that spot. Best of luck, pal."

These interactions went on for the next four months. It was winter in Colorado, so I'd often step off the bus into a foot of snow and walk down a cold sidewalk to my next prospect. I'd walk in, dust the snow off myself, and give them my speech. Yet over and over again, my prospects' initial enthusiasm about my willingness and positive attitude was quickly dampened when they learned about my record.

Unfazed, I stayed focused and reminded myself daily that the world owed me nothing. I would ask myself every single day, "How badly do I want it?" I knew that the answer was, "*Really* badly." I also knew that going back to my past was out of the question. Somewhere out there was a 10-year-old boy who deserved a father. But before I could fully be that father, I needed a place to live—and before I could get a place to live, *I needed a job!*

Giving up was not even remotely an option. I was undaunted by the literally hundreds of times I heard the word "no."

Then one day in April 2003, after four months of rejection, I walked into a financial services company that was looking for salespeople. I walked into the manager's office, sized him up and hit him with my best shot: "Hi, I'm Weldon Long. I just need one opportunity. One shot. Give me a chance, and I'll sell more of whatever you sell than anyone ever has. I'll never cheat or lie. I'll never complain about the economy or the leads. I just need a chance."

And like they always did, he said, "Well, we need more attitudes like that around here. Tell me more!"

"Well, there is a little more to the story. I spent 13 years in prison and right now I live in a halfway house . . ."

Only this time when I finished my story, the man said, "You know what? I think you are a changed man. I don't think you are the person your record says you are."

I thought I was hearing things! "Wha?" I stammered. "What did you just say?"

"I said I think you are a changed man. Let's talk a little more."

We spent a few minutes talking about sales and business development. I remember him saying something about how success in sales is about having a positive mindset and being able to handle rejection.

"Yeah," I thought to myself. "I got this."

After a few minutes, he walked out of the office to talk to someone else about me. While he was out of the office, I looked around and couldn't contain my excitement. Finally, I was going to have my chance to get a place, get my kid, and build my life. I paced the office and looked out over the parking lot. I imagined one of those cars was mine. (I had been riding the bus for four months in the cold and snow!)

After a few minutes the man came back in. "Hey, don't start thinking *this* office is yours yet," he joked.

I chuckled and said, "Aw, I'd be easy to work for."

He took out a pen and paper and started writing out the chronology of my criminal record as I recounted the dates and convictions. Once we finished, he left the room again. His excitement was contagious. I was so happy I thought I was going to explode!

After a few more minutes, he walked back into the office. Instantly I could see the disappointment on his face.

I looked him dead in the eye and said, "Don't say it! *Do not* say the word 'no' to me. Whatever comes out of your mouth next, *do not* let it be 'no.'"

"Weldon, if it was up to me, it would be 'yes,' but it's not up to me. With your record, there is just no way HR will hire you."

He sat down behind his desk, and I sat down across from him. I knew it wasn't his fault. I believed him. As I sat in the chair across from him, I began to feel a little overwhelmed. I wondered if I had been fooling myself all those years sitting in a cell and pretending I was something other than a pathetic loser.

We sat there quietly for a few moments. Then he looked at me and said the words that pierced me like an arrow. "What are you going to do?" he asked. It was the pity in his voice that brought me to my feet.

"What am I going to do? I am going to get a job and get a place to live and get my kid. Have you not heard a word I've said?" I was beginning to sound a little hysterical, but I couldn't help myself.

"Listen, if you've got a job, I want it. If you've got an opportunity, I need it. If you've got a chance, I'll take it. But *do not* give me your pity. I have been through far worse than this, pal. Do I have a job—yes or no?"

He could only stand there and shake his head.

I left his office without another word, rode the elevator downstairs, and walked out into a chilly Colorado evening. It was about 4:45 PM, and the sun had already settled behind Pikes Peak, immediately dropping the temperature into the 40s.

As I walked about a half-mile back to the bus stop, my mind began to panic. "Why did he feel sorry for me? What does he know that I don't know? Have I been deluding myself into thinking I could change my life by changing my thinking? Maybe the whole thing was a preposterous idea."

For the first time in years, I was scared shitless.

As I approached the concrete bus bench, I watched the cars stopped at the intersection. I could see the people in their warm cars, talking on the phone to friends and loved ones or listening to the radio. I looked off to the west at the homes nestled along the mountains. I could see the dim lights through the windows as dusk settled in. I imagined families behind those windows having dinner together or doing homework with the kids.

"Will I *ever* have that?" I wondered. "Or is that just a pipe dream conjured up by some hopeless convict to help him get through years behind bars?"

Suddenly I looked at my watch and realized it was well after 5 PM. The bus was late!

Now, anyone who takes a bus knows that being a few minutes late is not a big deal in the real world. However, I didn't live in the real world; I lived in a world under the authority of the Colorado Department of Corrections. And in that world, I had a 6 PM curfew for job hunting—and getting back late guaranteed a trip to the county jail and the possibility of a new felony for "escape." It was a very serious offense, with potentially disastrous consequences. Not getting a job would be the *least* of my problems.

By about 5:20 PM, full-scale desperation had set in. No one was ever going to see beyond my criminal history. The bus was late, and I was going to miss my curfew and get a trip to county jail or maybe worse. I wanted to cry right there at the bus stop. The pressure was becoming too much. The disappointment was too overwhelming.

Finally, the bus pulled up at 5:30. I jumped on and snapped at the driver, "Where the hell you been, man?"

"I've been working, driving this bus. Where *you* been?" he responded.

"I've been sitting on this bus bench freezing my ass off for 30 minutes. You're late!"

"I'm not late, buddy. I'm right on time," he said as he handed me the bus schedule.

I looked at it and realized he was right. I had misread the schedule. This bus ran at the bottom of the hour.

Feeling overwhelmed and beaten, I sat down and stared out the window. I knew it was going to be close to 6 PM by the time I got back to the halfway house. Maybe I would be on time; maybe I would be late. By that point, I almost didn't care.

When I stepped off the bus a couple of blocks from the halfway house, I started running as fast as I could, again looking like a madman running down the street in my four-month-old suit, carrying an empty briefcase.

I walked in the office and yelled over several guys waiting to check in, "Hey! Hey! Weldon Long here. Can somebody clock me in back there?"

I saw one of the halfway house staff look at me and grab my file. He stamped the time on my sheet and handed it back for me to sign. It read 5:58 PM. Whew. I had nothing but time.

I walked out of the office and down to my room, which I shared with six or eight other convicts. I sat on my bed, and my head fell into my hands. I started thinking about the guy who felt sorry for me an hour earlier. I started thinking about my life behind bars and how absurd it was to think I was going to walk out of the joint at nearly 40 years of age and build some imaginary dream-life.

Then I heard the words I had said to myself a thousand times before. "How badly do you want it, Mr. Long? Do you want it just a little bit, or do you want it more than you have ever wanted anything in your life?" I knew I wanted it badly and that the desperation I felt that day was just more fuel for the fire. It would strengthen me and reinforce my resolve to create something new and better for me and my son.

So I stood up. I stopped whining and feeling sorry for myself. I remembered something else I had said a million times: Stay focused. Never surrender. Success is closer than you think.

The next morning I got up, got dressed, hopped on the bus and made my first call. "Hi, I'm Weldon Long. I just need one opportunity. One shot. Give me a chance, and I'll sell more of whatever you sell than anyone ever has. I'll never cheat or lie. I'll never complain about the economy or the leads. I just need a chance."

April turned into May and May into June. I had been at this for six months and I was determined to find a job.

And then finally it happened. In June 2003, six months out of the joint, I walked into a small heating and air-conditioning company that was looking for a salesperson.

"Can you sell air conditioners?" the owner asked. I didn't know the first thing about air conditioners, but my desperation concealed my ignorance. "Of course I can sell them!"

Eventually I had to tell the owner the whole sordid story of my life. After I finished he said to me, "You know I am just not sure about you. You seem like a nice guy. But this record is pretty bad." He told me to call him in a few days.

And I did call him. In fact, I called him several times a day over the next two weeks. Finally, he said to me, "Dude, you are making me crazy!"

"Give me a job," I said, "And I'll be that persistent with customers."

He paused for a moment and said, "Okay. One chance, but that's it."

I started selling for him a few days later, and in my first month as a heating and air-conditioning salesman I sold $149,000 worth of air conditioners—one kitchen table at a time.

I worked that job for about a year and eventually decided to open my own company. Within five years of opening my own company I had grown sales to $20 million and earned a spot on *Inc.* magazine's list of fastest growing companies in America. I didn't know anything about the heating and air-conditioning industry, but I knew how to sell. And, after all, nothing happens until something gets sold—right? Not bad for a three-time loser and high-school dropout. Not bad at all.

I got a place to live and my little boy got the father he deserved. As I write these words, I am on Maui with my son, Hunter, and his girlfriend, Matti. He just finished his first year of college, and he is planning for his future. Over the past few years, I have had the privilege of meeting and speaking with some of the same men whose books lighted the path for me, including the late Dr. Stephen R. Covey, Mark Victor Hansen, and the incomparable builder of sales champions, Tom Hopkins. I have had the honor of developing customized sales and prosperity mindset training programs for some of America's greatest companies.

Henry David Thoreau once said, "If we advance confidently in the directions of our own dreams and endeavor to live the life we have imagined, we will meet with success unexpected in common hours."

I suppose in many ways my success has been "unexpected," but in my mind, it was not. I saw it, and I put it in my box. Over the years, through a million choices, attitudes, and beliefs, I pulled this new life out my box. After all, you just can't put a life of wealth, happiness, and prosperity in the box and accidentally create something else.

The universe doesn't work that way.

As I said in the beginning, this book is not meant to be the definitive word on sales or positive thinking or anything else for that matter. There are people a lot smarter than me for that. This is simply the story of one man's experience. These are merely the lessons I have learned and how they have affected my life and business.

I am an average guy living an extraordinary life as a result of learning and implementing these simple ideas. I am riding the wave, but I understand full well I didn't create the ocean. *The Power of Consistency* changed everything in my life and business.

However, I do know this: To succeed in life and business, you need to be more than smart and ambitious. It requires more than understanding human nature and the sales process.

It takes consistency.

Success in life and business requires understanding that if you change your *thoughts*, you will change your *emotions*. If you change your *emotions*, you will change your *actions*. And if you change your *actions*, you will change your *results*.

After all, it's not rocket science.

INDEX